"GUIDRY, YOU WILL NEVER BE ABLE TO PITCH IN THIS LEAGUE."
Yankee owner George Steinbrenner

"I KEPT HAVING NIGHTMARES . . .
Going into my windup, rearing back, making the big kick, and on my follow-through having my left arm fly right off my body and go spinning into space."

Not for a long time have we had a baseball book so charged with spirit and courage and the roaring excitement of the game.

"WARM AND WELL WRITTEN."
Washington Post

"RON GUIDRY OFFERS SOME THINGS NOT FOUND IN MOST BASEBALL BIOGRAPHIES . . .
He remembers the tough years before stardom . . . and old-time family values."
Philadelphia Bulletin

Guidry

BY RON GUIDRY
& PETER GOLENBOCK

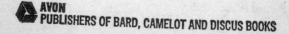

AVON
PUBLISHERS OF BARD, CAMELOT AND DISCUS BOOKS

AVON BOOKS
A division of
The Hearst Corporation
959 Eighth Avenue
New York, New York 10019

Copyright © 1980 by Ron Guidry and Peter Golenbock
Published by arrangement with Prentice-Hall, Inc.
Library of Congress Catalog Card Number: 80-13732
ISBN: 0-380-55137-3

The Prentice-Hall Inc., edition contains the following
Library of Congress Cataloging in Publication Data:

Guidry, Ron, date
    Guidry.
    1. Guidry, Ron, date   2. Baseball payers—
United States—Biography. I. Golenbock, Peter, date
joint author.

First Avon Printing, May, 1981

Contents

To My Wife Bonnie,
Daughter Jamie,
and the Little One on the Way—R.G.

To My Little Miss Wish—P.G.

Foreword

While working on *The Bronx Zoo*, which chronicled the 1978 Yankee season of craziness and strife, there was one day after another of controversy. If Reggie Jackson wasn't feuding with then manager Billy Martin, then Thurman Munson was feuding with the reporters, or another player was feuding with Yankee owner George Steinbrenner.

Amidst the storms, there always seemed to be an aura of tranquillity surrounding one of the lockers, that of pitcher Ron Guidry. Every fourth or fifth day Guidry would go out to the mound, and twenty-seven out of thirty times that year he would return a winner, and after the game reporters would make small talk, ask him how his arm was or ask him about a certain play, and with great deliberation and politeness, Guidry would patiently answer all their questions and go about his business. I couldn't help but notice that there was a serenity about Guidry that seemed out of place on the Yankees or even in New York City's helter-skelter society. I determined then that I would attempt to discover what it was in his background that made Ron Guidry the way he is, both on and off the field.

One ingredient contributing to his success is that behind his calm exterior burns a fierce competitor, and whenever Ron Guidry has been faced with a challenge he has responded to meet it. The night he was born, August 28, 1950, his father, Roland, who at the time weighed about 130 pounds soaking wet, was pacing back and forth in the hospital waiting room when another man, about six-foot-three and 220 pounds, started bragging about his newborn son. "He weighs seven pounds six ounces, going to be quite a kid," the man was saying. Mr. Guidry stood there listening, annoyed by the man's bragging but too polite to say anything. It would not be long before his own child would be born.

Ronald Ames weighed in at eight pounds when he was born, and immediately Proud Papa Guidry went to find the man in the waiting room to do a little bragging of his own. Unfortunately, the man was gone. Nevertheless, on his birthday, Ronald Ames Guidry had met his first challenge and he has continued to do so to this day.

I used to love to watch Whitey Ford and Sandy Koufax pitch—the former because he was so clever, the latter because he was so overpowering. But most of all I used to enjoy watching them because I knew that when the game was over, each would inevitably walk off the mound a winner. Koufax retired in 1966 and Ford in 1967, and it's been nearly a decade for another pitcher of their ilk to come onto the scene. When I sat in Yankee Stadium watching Guidry strike out 18 California Angels I couldn't help thinking that barring an arm injury this self-effacing, almost shy, skinny left-hander with the brooding face might someday challenge Lefty Grove, Warren Spahn, Ford, and Koufax for the honor of being recognized as the greatest left-handed pitcher the game has ever seen.

Guidry is self-confident without being arrogant and possesses a cool head on his shoulders. It goes without saying that he's a great athlete.

One wintry Louisiana afternoon Ronnie and I played touch football in a park for hours with a group of young kids who were lucky enough to be there. To play touch against Ronnie is a losing proposition, and I learned that early in the game. He was playing quarterback, which is good, because you have a chance to win if his receivers drop enough of his pinpoint passes. (If he plays end, you have to hope the quarterback has an erratic arm.) Anyway, Ronnie dropped back to pass, and when he saw his receivers were covered, he started to run. He came within two feet of where I was planted,

10

but when I went for him I grabbed air. He had darted away so fast. I could only stand there, turn around, and watch as he flitted back and forth, in and out, until he reached the goal line.

"It's not fair," I said to myself. "How can anybody be that quick . . . be so good?" Then I thought of the 18-strikeout game against the Angels. "Now I know how they must have felt," I thought.

One of the joys of doing this book was my opportunity to travel to Louisiana's Cajun country to visit with Ronnie, his wife Bonnie, and their friends and relatives. As a Northerner, and a metropolitan New Yorker, I am used to living with crowds, noise, pollution, and an internal motor that is always racing. After a couple days in Lafayette, with no crowds or noise, little pollution, and my motor down to an idle, I was suffering from culture shock in my own country. It didn't take very long to get used to—no, make that enjoy—the slower, more easygoing lifestyle. I came to value the pleasures and peacefulness of ambling through the woods in search of (that day) reclusive fowl. I enjoyed watching the Cajun lifestyle with its emphasis on mutual respect, courteousness, and camaraderie. Loved hearing Grandpa Gus in his thick Cajun drawl spin his stories and seeing Travis Guidry, Ronnie's thirteen-year-old retarded brother, showered with love, and drinking Grace Guidry's coffee and eating Bonnie's mom's cooking.

A warning about the Cajun food: It's not for the meek.

One evening Bonnie's mom, who is an expert cook, fixed some Chicken and Sausage Gumbo and a dozen ducks the way Ronnie likes them cooked (the recipe of which you'll find in the appendix), and after the meal, which was delicious, the onions and garlic in the stuffing gave me the worst case of heartburn I'd ever had in my whole life. "Mrs. Matthews," I burped, "I need Alka-Seltzer, and I need it fast. I've never had heartburn this bad."

11

She had seen how much I had eaten, and she smiled at me. "Oh, thank you," she said in all sincerity. "That's the nicest compliment I've ever gotten."

What struck me most of all while visiting was a feeling that there is great contentedness in Ron Guidry's world. He is truly happy living where he is, with his people, and he enjoys doing what he does in his surroundings. He is at peace, and there aren't many people on earth who can say that.

Ron Guidry did not have to become a star baseball player to find happiness. He merely brought it with him to the world of baseball.

I would like to take this opportunity to thank the following people for aiding in the creation of this book: Roland, Grace, Gus, Gladys and Bonnie Guidry, James Broussard, Bobby and Kathy Badeaux, Ray Boudreau, Felton Trahan, Bob Banna, Sonny Roy, Tigue Moore, Boo Menard, Richard Conques, and John Schneider for inviting me into their homes and offices and giving their valuable time; my agent, Edward J. Acton, and Doug Newton, Eddie Sapir, and Mr. Schneider for helping to arrange the collaboration; Kathy Ducote for her help in setting up the interviews; Alexa Pierce and Susan Heller for assisting in the tape transcriptions; Wayne Coffee for his valuable assistance in organizing the material; Rhonda Sonnenberg for her valuable editorial assistance; Nick D'Incecco of Prentice-Hall for giving me my start in this business; and finally Ronnie Guidry, a great athlete and a special person.

Peter Golenbock
Englewood, N.J.

"Thank God I'm a country boy."

John Martin Sommers

1

Mom Didn't Like It, but I Played

My mom didn't want me to be a ballplayer. When I was very young her brother, Boulon, who was a pitcher, was hit on the shin by a line drive, and he was in the hospital a long time. Then a couple years later one of the local boys was pitching, and the batter hit one back at him, hit him above the heart, and he died. My mom never forgot that, so out of respect for her wishes I didn't touch a baseball until I was seven.

I was very small for my age, and that was another reason Mom didn't want me playing. I didn't weigh more than ninety pounds for the longest while, a skinny kid, brittle-looking. I always enjoyed watching baseball, but because Mom didn't want me to play, I wouldn't.

Our home was three blocks from the park where all the kids played, and one afternoon I walked over there just to see what was going on. Kids were having a Little League practice. They were scattered all over the field, and as I walked around the edge of the field, I could see their coach hitting flies to the outfielders. First he'd hit one to the leftfielder, then the centerfielder, then the rightfielder, and the kids would run down the balls and throw them in.

As I was making my way from center field to left field, the coach hit a ball to left field. The kid in left stumbled and fell going back for the ball, which bounced, took a short hop, and rolled another twenty feet to where I was walking. As I bent over to pick it up, I could hear all the kids shouting, "Throw the ball in. Hey, kid, throw it in," and so with all my might I threw it in. I was seven years old, about as tall and skinny as a broomstick, but when I let that ball fly I discovered I could do it easily. I later figured out that it was about 250 feet from where I had been standing to home plate. When I let fly, the ball sailed over the heads of the infielders and the catcher and the coach and rattled against the top of the backstop.

When it happened I didn't think much about it, but I became scared when two of the coaches came running after me. I didn't know what I had done, but I thought

I did something wrong. I was little, and they were big, and they were running after me, fast. I didn't know what they were going to do. I froze.

This one coach came over, and he was huffing and puffing, and what he said was, "What's your name?"

"Ronnie Guidry, sir."

"Do you like baseball, son?"

"Oh, yes, sir," I said, "but I can't play. My mommy won't let me."

"Are you Roland's son?" he asked.

"Yes, sir," I said.

"I'll talk to your daddy," he said.

"Yes, sir," I said.

After the coach went back to practice, one of our neighbors, Roy Menard, came over to talk to me about playing on the team. He said he thought I could help the team, and he also said he'd talk to my daddy about it.

A couple days later my dad asked me if I wanted to play ball. I told him I thought it was something I'd like to do, but I also told him how Mom felt about it. "What about Momma?" I said.

He rubbed his chin and made a face. "You go ahead and play and I'll take care of that when the time comes." The next day my dad took me shopping for a glove. In those days a good glove cost four or five dollars. I fell in love with one that cost fifteen. But Dad bought it for me. We may not have been wealthy, but whenever I needed something, my dad always found a way to get it.

My dad and I agreed that we wouldn't tell Momma about my playing until the first game. I would practice in secret, telling Mom I was going over to Granddad's house when I was really going over to the park. The day of the first game my heart was doing somersaults.

I was in my room and dressed quickly. I put on the yellow Southern Bell Half-pints shirt and then the pants and the shoes, and taking a deep breath I went out to confront Mom. She was doing the dishes, and when I walked out there and she saw me, her mouth dropped.

19

"What in the world?" she said.

"Will you come to see my ballgame, Momma?" I said.

She couldn't believe it. "Your ballgame? What ballgame? You don't know how to play ball."

"Yes I do, Momma," I said. "I've been practicing for a month at the park." I grinned.

She gave me one of her stern looks, as only she could. "No, Ronnie. I don't want you doing this. You'll get hurt," she said.

"I've been practicing every day and I haven't gotten hurt yet," I argued. "There's more chance of my being hurt by crossing the street or getting hit by lightning. Come see what it's like, Momma, please come."

Before she could answer, Dad walked in. "I think it would be good for the boy," he said. "And besides, he wants to play so badly I don't see how you can have the heart to stop him."

She scowled at me, then at Dad, and then she put her hands on her hips, shook her head, and broke out into a grin. "Okay," she said, "I'll go to the game."

And she went, too, except that she didn't sit in the stands. Afraid to watch during the entire game, she sat in the car. Every time the crowd started hollering, she would shudder, then look out the window to see if I was all right, because she was sure that each time the crowd made noise I had gotten hurt. That first year she spent most of the games sitting in the car, on the one hand curious to see what was going on, but on the other afraid to watch.

It was a year later before I got to pitch. I played center and right field, and Mom didn't mind that because in the outfield I was so far away from the batter. She'd watch the game when I was out in the field. At bat, though, she still wouldn't look. I had a very strong arm for such a small kid, and the coach and the other players wanted me to pitch, but I knew Momma wouldn't let me because of what had happened to her brother. Nevertheless, our team was playing a very important game, and by mid-game we were losing something like 10–7, and we were out of pitchers. The other players on the team really wanted me to pitch bad. They knew I had a good arm, and they figured if I pitched we'd have a chance because we had a good hitting team. The other kids were begging my dad to let me pitch, but he wouldn't give in. Mom was sitting in the car, and he just wouldn't let me pitch. An inning later the score was 14–7, theirs, and the coach spoke to my dad about my pitching in the game. I didn't know this at the time, but my dad told the other players, "I'm going to put my neck on the line. I'll let you put Ronnie on the mound, but you have to win the game. If you don't win, Ronnie's going to be through as a ballplayer, because his mother will forbid him to play again. But if you win, I think I can convince her how important Ronnie is to the team."

When I got on that mound, I felt right at home. I found I had great control as a kid and with my strong left arm, they didn't score again. Fortunately, we tied the score and won by two runs, and I was allowed to keep pitching.

My parents were always so great about backing me. It meant the world to me that they would come and watch my games. And yet, as I look back on it, as much as they supported and encouraged me, they never once pushed me or preached to me. Whatever I wanted to do, they were behind me a hundred percent. If I had come home and said, "I don't want to play anymore," they would have said, "Whatever you want, Ronnie, is fine with us."

As I went on in organized ball, I came to appreciate my parents' attitude more and more. I saw kids whose parents pushed them mercilessly, which is one of the worst things you can do to a kid. A kid gets to be fifteen and six-foot-two and fast and immediately his dad starts pressing him to go out for the football team. Maybe the kid doesn't want to play football. Maybe he wants to be an artist, yet the parent is saying, "You ought to go out for football and win a scholarship." Then if the kid doesn't go out, or if he goes out and doesn't get the scholarship, he feels he's disappointed his parents. And all along he's played football and hasn't enjoyed a minute of it. If he doesn't get the scholarship, he's wasted all those years doing something he hates, and he's getting a late start doing what it is he really loves. It's a terrible thing to do to a child.

How many artists, jugglers, piano players, and dancers have been lost to the world because a parent pushed a kid to be an athlete? The child then drops out of sports, and it's too late for him to develop into anything. If a kid wants to do something, whatever it is, I believe the parent should just back him. Whether he wants to be an attorney, or a dancer, or a president, or a janitor—if that's what he's content with, leave him alone and back him. Too often the kid will end up resenting the parent, and soon the kid goes off on his separate way.

Parents should take a real interest in the activities the child does enjoy. But there is a right way and a wrong way of offering encouragement.

The most terrible thing I've seen parents do to their kid is ridicule them if they make an error or strike out, to always bring up the bad points. Nobody feels worse about not performing well than the kid himself. I've heard parents tell their kid, "Hey, sport, tell Mr. Smith how you struck out yesterday with the bases loaded." How's the kid supposed to feel about that? I've seen adults get drunk and run out into the street in their underwear, and yet no one would dare say anything because it would be tasteless to embarrass an adult. But that same person wouldn't be ashamed at all to embarrass his own kid.

Because of my parents, all my memories of Little League were positive. I can't tell you how many other kids quit baseball because of the pressure put on them by their parents. It all traces back to the distorted emphasis people place on winning. In every junior high school locker room in the country is plastered the sign, "Winning isn't everything. It's the only thing." For a pro ballplayer, that may be so. For a young kid, that's ridiculous. Nobody wins all the time, especially in baseball. I don't care who you are or what you do, you have to lose sometime. It's part of being human.

Certainly winning is fun. It's the greatest thing in the world, and it should be your goal when you set out to do something. But you also have to be able to accept losing. You have to be able to say, "I lost, and that's all there is to it." It's not that the other guy or the other team is necessarily better. Just, "I lost today." You accept it, live with it, and you resolve that you'll come back tomorrow and try even harder. And this is true in every field, not just in sports. It's not the winning that's so important. What is important is to be able to know in your heart that you did the best you could. I can honestly say that I don't know of a better competitor than me, and I *can* accept losing.

I've had to. Although I've been fortunate to win many more times than I've lost in my major league career, some of those losses could have weighed heavily on my mind if I would have allowed it. I did not.

It's hard for me to imagine anyone growing up in a better family environment than I did. My parents, my grandparents, my many other relatives, everyone showed me such love and respect, I grew up giving that love and respect back to them. They gave me many of the material things I wanted, but they didn't spoil me. The biggest thing of all, though they probably don't realize it, was that they were so supportive. Within reason, I was always allowed to do what I wanted. There was no pressure on me to be a ballplayer or a carpenter or a doctor. If I wanted to spend my time digging ditches or playing the drums, that was fine with them so long as I was happy.

My daddy would always tell me, "Ronnie, you do whatever you want to do, but whatever it is you give it

everything you've got." And for as long as I can remember, whenever I've gotten involved in something,
even something others would consider insignificant, I've
always gone all the way. As a little kid, I was into
building plastic model ships. It wasn't enough just to
build two or three. I wanted to build a model of each
ship in the U.S. Atlantic and Pacific fleets, and before I
was finished, I did just that. I also had two fleets "in
mothballs," more than a hundred models in all. Finally,
I decided I didn't want to build model ships anymore. I
had a new love. Drums.

When I started playing the drums, I practiced day
and night. I wanted to be the world's best drummer.
And when my grandpa Gus introduced me to hunting, I
became addicted to it. And I still am. It was the same
way when I started playing ball. Once I began playing,
I decided I was going to be a major league ballplayer. I
can remember when the Yankees were playing in the
World Series in the early 1960's. Momma didn't watch
baseball during the regular season, but she used to
watch every game of the World Series. I was about ten
years old, and she and I were sitting in the den watching the TV, and I said to her, "Do you see those fellas
on the TV?" and I'd point out Mantle and Maris and
Whitey Ford. "I'm going to be up there one of these
days." My momma would say, "Oh, Ronnie, sure you
are." And I said, "You're gonna see, Momma. You're
gonna see what I can do. I'm going to play with them
and make me some money and get me a nice little car."
Momma, she would look at me and smile.

To look at me, you wouldn't believe I could throw as
hard as I can. You don't, however, have to be well-built
to throw a good fastball. You need strong legs, an effi-
cient, compact windup, and a long arm that will supply
a lot of leverage. I have all three.

Ever since I first started playing ball, I was constantly surprising people with my speed. Once when I
was about thirteen I was playing in our Colt League

and pitching on the sidelines to my Uncle Boulon. He had been a great pitcher himself until that line drive nailed him on the shin, and he was an experienced catcher. I threw Boulon a half-dozen fastballs, at which point he remembered that he had forgotten to run some unnamed errands. At the time I didn't think anything of it. Later he told me he couldn't even see the ball. He didn't want to embarrass himself. "Right then I knew Ronnie had the ability to go a long way," he says.

I had one other physical attribute that I've always been proud of. I can run like the wind. I often wonder just how good a major league outfielder I could have been. A lot of scouts have said I could have made the majors as an outfielder. Other ballplayers have said the same thing. To tell you the truth, I think there are very few outfielders in the majors who are better than me right now. That sounds cocky, but I'm not just mouthing off. I know what I can do, and after being in the majors a few years, I know how I rate. I've got a live arm. I can run a 4.2 forty and a 9.7 hundred, and as for my timing and reflexes, only once in my whole pitching career have I ever been hit by a batted ball. Plus I can hit. Whenever I played I hit well. I was the leadoff batter or the number-two man, and I hit about .350 every year.

I'm funny in one way. My last three years as a pitcher for the Yankees, I've had a 59–18 won-lost record, but I still fantasize about playing the outfield in the majors. If Babe Ruth could do it . . .

I did, in fact, get to play out my fantasy for one-third of an inning last year. There were two outs in the ninth inning, Tommy John was pitching, and Billy Martin was bringing in Don Hood in relief, and rather than go to the mound himself, Billy called me over and told me to go out there and call Hood to the mound. I had been pestering Billy to let me play outfield in the late innings of a game, and after he told me to relieve John with Hood, he said, "After you do that, go out to center field and replace Bobby Murcer." I grabbed my glove, went out to the mound to talk to Tommy, and finally the ump came over and said, "What are you going to do, kid?" I wigwagged my fingers for Hood to come in, then I pointed to center field. "I'm in for Murcer," I told the ump, and I ran out there. When Bob Sheppard made the announcement over the loudspeaker, I got one of the biggest ovations ever. Unfortunately, the final batter grounded out.

The next day, the last day of the season, Billy told me he would have let me go out there again, but the ground was wet, and he didn't want to take any chance of my getting hurt.

Some of my greatest childhood memories come from doing things other than pitching. I always loved to hit. Even more, I love to run the bases. One of my best friends is a fellow by the name of Bobby Badeaux. We were teammates on our American Legion team. My wife is best friends with his wife. He'd stay over my house and we'd hunt together, play ball together, and eat potato-chip sandwiches and drink Dr. Pepper together. We're still very close, and when we played ball we used to love to drive the other team crazy with our speed.

Bobby was even faster than I was, and we'd have base-stealing contests. We both felt that the only way to steal a base was standing up. If you had to slide, you just couldn't cut it. A lot of times we'd both be on base, and that's when we'd try to drive the opposing pitchers crazy. We'd pull double steals, delayed steals, take the extra base. We loved to run. One time we almost outsmarted ourselves.

We were losing 8–2 in the bottom of the ninth. This was American Legion ball, so I'd say we were seventeen years old. We scored 3 runs to close the score to 8–5. Then a teammate hit a single and Bobby dragged a bunt for a hit. I also drag-bunted for a hit. The bases were loaded, and the next guy walked to make the score 8–6. Bobby moved to third and I went to second with the tying run.

There were two outs, but I knew there was no way

26

we were going to lose that game. Their confidence was shaken. They were coming apart at the seams, and with our bench and fans riding them, I could almost hear their prayers for a third out.

Of course, Bobby and I were doing everything we could to make it worse for them. With the bases loaded, their pitcher was taking a full windup, and as he'd go into his motion, Bobby and I would practically run down to the next base before coming back. Their catcher wasn't about to throw the ball to try to pick us off, and with every pitch I was coming closer and closer to third as the pitcher delivered the ball. The crowd was on its feet screaming, and we were racing back and forth like madmen, and I knew it was only a matter of time before the pressure would break them.

When the pitcher threw again, Bobby and I took off. This time the batter hit a weak grounder to the third baseman. All he had to do was step on third or throw to first and they'd have won, but instead he threw home trying to force Bobby at the plate. The ball hit Bobby in the helmet and rolled away, and when I saw this I touched third and came home in a cloud of dust, sliding in seconds behind Bobby, who was getting up from his own slide. Together we walked back to the bench.

Suddenly our coach called time-out. "Hey, where the hell is Ronnie?" he was yelling. "Why isn't Ronnie on third base?" Someone else was standing on third. Bobbie and I were sitting at the end of the bench watching the coach. It had been so quick the umpire had failed to count my run. The ump finally saw me sitting in the dugout and said, "Gentlemen, I'm faced with indecision. I never saw the run score. How can I say that he scored?"

I yelled out, "Ask the first-base ump." Fortunately, he had seen what happened, so the run counted. And we won the game.

One way or another, Bobby and I always managed to find ways to have fun out on the field. Whenever I didn't pitch, I'd be in left, he in center, and during the whole game we'd talk back and forth about everything:

27

Girls, food, cars, hunting, our futures. You name it, we discussed it. Occasionally our discussions would be interrupted.

"Whatcha doin' tonight? Gotta date?" he'd yell over.

"Yeah, I do."

"Where ya goin'?"

"Not sure. I think maybe we'll go to the show," and then the ball would be hit our way and we'd look up to try to locate it, and then we'd discuss which of us would catch it. "You want this one?"

Bobby'd say, "Nah, you take it. I got the last one."

"Okay."

We believed we were so good that sometimes we'd lazily jog after the ball and then put on a burst of speed to make a diving catch. Once the batter hit a line drive deep toward the left-center-field alley. The runner on first happened to be a bitter enemy of Bobby's—they were dating the same girl. Bobby wanted to get him badly, wanted to throw him out or double him off, do something to show him up. The ball was to me, but Bobby wanted it badly, so I circled behind him to let him have his way. Bobby had to run a long way for the ball, and in his haste he jumped a second too early for it with the ball just coming down over his glove. Though I was backing up, before I could react, the ball hit me in the chest and fell to the ground. I picked it up and everyone was screaming for me to throw home. Bobby's nemesis was rounding second and heading home with the winning run, but as I was about to throw, Bobby growled, "Gimme that ball." He snatched it from my hand, fired a perfect strike to the relay man, who made a perfect throw home to nail the guy at the plate.

"That'll show him," Bobby said as we trotted off the field. Our coach was scowling at us as we came into the dugout, but what could he say?

Still, what I did best was pitch. There was something about standing on that mound, one-on-one with the batter, fiercely intense, that I've always loved. It was my coaches and teammates who first put me on the mound, not me. I just went along with it. That's the kind of kid I was. If they had wanted me to be the first-base coach, that would have been fine with me.

Even as a four-foot-five fifty-pounder, I could really throw smoke. I was the smallest kid on the team, and yet I could shoot bullets. As a kid I enjoyed great success, though it wasn't until I was about fifteen that people really started to notice me. About that time, the local baseball fans started talking about "the skinny kid who threw smoke." And I *was* skinny. I didn't weigh more than 125. But it was a hard 125. I was deceptively strong, as I am now. Catfish Hunter'll tell you. I like to use the weight room we have at Yankee Stadium, and one day I was doing one-arm curls with my usual amount of weight—one hundred pounds. I finished, and Cat walked in and went over to the machine. He could barely budge it, and he's a lot bigger than I am.

"Damn," he said, "who's been working out with this?" I merely smiled.

My biggest thrill in youth baseball was reaching the finals of the state tournament. I was the pitcher and Bobby was my catcher, and we swept into the championship game, where we faced a pitcher by the name of Kenny Alfred. Alfred was getting a lot of ink, and everyone was saying he was the best pitcher of our age group in the state—everyone, of course, except me. I didn't give a darn about the publicity. Still don't. But I was excited about pitching against Alfred. I had an additional challenge, and in the game I pitched a shutout, struck out 15, and we won something like 7 to 0.

The next year we drove to Beaumont, Texas, to play in the regional championships, and at the tender age of fourteen I learned a very important lesson: Don't fool around before a big game.

Our trip was memorable, but not for anything we did on the field. We were excited about getting away from Lafayette and spending the weekend in a big city. We thought we were going to stay in a fancy hotel, but when we got there, it turned out we were bunking in the local YMCA, twenty-five guys in a room, cots covering every inch of floor space.

We got in bed, and as soon as the lights went out the fun began. We were throwing pillows and towels and squirting shaving cream, which we had brought along for that purpose, as few of us shaved. One of our players, Howard, was the team clown. He never stopped. Once when he was pitching he got hit with a shot back to the box and collapsed on the mound. The crowd hushed and everyone ran out to see if he was seriously hurt. He looked like he was unconscious, until he slowly opened his eyes and looked at our manager. "How's the crowd taking it!" Howard asked.

Howard was on the other side of the room. A shaving-cream filled towel had just whizzed between Bobby and me, and I picked it up, tied it into a tight knot, and sprayed it with a heavy gob of my own shaving cream. In the light from the hallway I could see Howard's shadow, and when he was in the open, I let that towel fly. I could hear the *smack* against someone's face—not Howard's. In the middle of the room, just as I threw the towel, someone had sat up. We turned the lights on and discovered Flavius Martin, an elderly, local baseball fan who went with us wherever we went, lying flat on his back with the soggy towel across his face. We thought it was hysterical, until we noticed that Flavius hadn't moved. I was worried I had killed the guy with the towel, but then he started snoring, and we breathed easier. Later I sprayed shaving cream all over Howard's pillow. He climbed into bed, put his head facedown onto the pillow. He looked like he had been hit in the face with a cream pie.

Later, about six of us sneaked out of the room and went looking for the swimming pool to take a midnight dip. We couldn't find it, so we went outside and roamed the streets of Beaumont until four in the morning.

Our game was scheduled for nine the next morning,

and when we took the field we were hurting. Got beat bad. The next night we got to sleep on time. It was a double elimination tournament, and I pitched, but they scored a run in the ninth on an error, and we lost 1–0 and were eliminated. We lost, but we shouldn't have. And I vowed it would never happen again. All the fun we had had wasn't worth our getting beat.

2

Hunting with My Shoe and Other Bayou Country Stories

Before I started playing ball I was a loner. There just weren't many kids to play with. Not that I needed any. I was always comfortable with myself. I could sit up in a tree house for five hours and be content. I had a dog, and the dog gave me enjoyment. Around the time I first played Little League is when I started associating with other kids. A couple of my teammates were from the country, and they had been hunting, and I wondered to myself, "What the heck is hunting?" So I asked my dad and he told me.

Where I come from hunting is a way of life. The boys start to hunt about the same time they start playing ball.

I remember the first time I went hunting with Grandpa Gus. Gus was one of thirteen kids, and he worked hard for everything he got. He would work twenty hours a day in the fields to make a dollar or drive a truck across the country to make forty dollars a week. In his spare time he loved to hunt, and I was the only grandson, and he loved to take me with him when he hunted.

I was eight or nine the first time I went duck hunting with Gus. You can imagine a young child sitting in a blind, unaccustomed to what's going to happen. I sat there with him early in the twilight, waiting for that first flutter of wings, that very, very fast movement distinguishing the ducks from other birds. As we sat there, he kept telling me, "Get ready when I tell you. You're gonna hear 'em." I never doubted his word. He said I was going to hear them, and I believed him. I was tense, waiting, eager, my shell in my single-shot gun, my arm propped up, and all of a sudden I see these tiny specks in front of me. Gus says, "Ronnie, shoot, they're ducks." *Boom*, he shot, and *boom*, I shot, and I actually hit a duck, which was probably the happiest moment of my young life. He went out to retrieve the ducks and came back with my duck and two other ducks. "How did you shoot two?" I asked. "I didn't hear you shoot twice."

He said, "I shot a second shot the same instant you shot your shot." I said to myself, "How can he get two ducks with two shots?" I was impressed, proud of my grandpa. But in my own mind I was determined to be an even better shot than he was, and I told him so. "We'll see about that," he said, and from that time on we started playing games, seeing who was the better shot.

Later on that day Gus said to me, "Let's see who can bring a duck down closest to the blind." The ducks came, and he shot, and a duck fell within fifty feet of us, and he was bragging, laughing, and he said, "Let's see you top that." And now remember, this was the first time I'd ever been duck hunting, and I'm sitting there and all of a sudden I heard a whirr overhead and fired the gun, and a duck fell right into the blind! Gus laughs about that to this day!

My Aunt Dixie used to own a lot of land with good woods for hunting, and every Saturday or Sunday Momma or Grandpa would take me over there to hunt with my BB gun. As I told you, Momma was always afraid of my getting hurt, and it was no different with hunting. She'd say, "Okay, Ronnie, you can go ahead back there, but I'll call you every ten or fifteen minutes, and when you hear me calling you, you come out of those woods, wave your hand, and that'll tell me everything is all right." Mom would stand out on Aunt Dixie's back porch and she'd stare out into the woods looking for me, and she'd start hollering, "RONNNNNNN-ALD." She'd call maybe two or three times, and I'd hear her and no matter whether I was just about to shoot or not, I'd have to come running as fast as I could to the edge of the woods and wave back to her.

Once, when we were driving back home, I got mad. I had had enough. I said, "Momma, when are you going to let me hunt in peace? Just let me go back there and hunt. I'm about ready to shoot something, I'm looking right down the barrel at it, and you start calling."

Mom said, "Ronald, you know I just want to see if you're okay."

I said, "I'll be okay. If I shoot myself, I'll crawl back to the house. I'm not going to kill myself with a BB gun. Leave me alone." But of course she wouldn't. She was so afraid of my getting hurt.

Grandpa Gus had a 410 shotgun that he let me use every time we went out into the fields together. He started me out slow. First we hunted doves and finally, when I got to hitting them, we went duck hunting. And after we did this for a while Grandpa said, "I have no need for the 410 anymore. I will give it to you as a present." It was a single shot, and I hunted with that until I was about twelve. I went all over the area. I had different relatives, and I'd go hunt with them. I got to be a pretty good shot with the 410, but then I got tired of having to reload so many times, so I told my dad and he lent me his gun, which allowed for three shots at a time, and I used that until I signed my first professional contract. Then I bought my dad a gun. When I hunted, I used that. Never had a gun of my own until two years ago. Now I let everyone use mine.

My daddy worked for the railroad weekends, so usually it was Gus who took me out. Gus taught me everything I know about hunting. He gave me all the knowledge and the patience I needed to hunt. He showed me that if you waited long enough, your patience would be rewarded. He showed me how I could wait five hours for a duck before getting him, and the same thing goes for baseball. That's why I have the ability to wait, wait, wait, wait, wait all day long for one pitch to get a guy out.

Gus taught me everything about the different kinds of birds. He showed me the right way to set up a duck blind. It's built near water and should be about seven feet long and three feet wide. You camouflage it with underbrush and weeds, put a little seat in it, and you make a little ditch in front of you for your shells, and you set up a rack for your gun. After building the blind, you set your duck decoys out into the water. The bigger the body of water, the more decoys you put out there.

Gus taught me that good hunters don't shoot at ducks once they land on the water, because that's not sport. If you're hungry and ducks are scarce, then it's okay, but ordinarily you wait for the ducks to land and scare them up, then while they take off you shoot at them.

I learned that different birds act differently. Pintail ducks, for instance, are wary birds that fly very high. Mallards you can call in if you have a good duck caller. The wood duck, which is not normally shot from a blind but in the woods, is a colorful bird that hides in its cover until you're almost on top of it. Then, when you flush it out, it takes off like a knuckleball. You have to shoot quick before it starts bobbing and weaving, and it's usually a thickly wooded area so that more often than not when you swing your gun around to shoot at it, you bump into a tree.

There's a practical reason why a hunter needs to be able to pick out the kind of bird coming in before shooting at it. In Louisiana a hunter can shoot one hundred points worth of ducks in a day. The most numerous ducks, like the pintails, teals, gray ducks, and widgins, are classified as ten-point ducks. Mallards are numerous, but they're valued for their green heads; therefore a lot of hunters go after them. The mallard drake has a twenty-five-point value, a hen, seventy points. They limit the hens more to protect the breed. Wood ducks, probably the prettiest ducks in America, are rated at seventy points, and a canvasback, which is an uncommon duck, is rated at one hundred.

Fortunately for many hunters, the law states that the last duck you shoot determines your legal limit. In other words, if you shoot nine ten-point ducks and then shoot a canvasback, you'd still be okay with the game warden. A hunter does not want to wake up at four in the morning, drive out to the blind, take one shot at six o'clock only to find out it's a canvasback, and then go home. That doesn't make for a very exciting day.

Once I was with my dad and my cousin, whose name

37

is also Ronald Guidry, though everyone calls him Joe. We began early in the morning and were hunting for more than an hour when the sun finally rose. From a distance we saw two ducks. We couldn't make out what they were, but Dad said, "Shoot them anyway," so I shot both of them. When we retrieved them we realized they were canvasbacks. Luckily, there were three of us, and going under the assumption we shot them last, we still were able to end up with a decent day's hunting. If there had only been two of us out there, the day's hunting would have been over quickly.

Gus also taught me about other different animals and how to hunt them. He taught me about hunting rabbits, frogs, and alligators. For instance, he was always telling me how when he was a kid he would hunt rabbits with a stick. It was easier to hunt in his day. There were fewer hunters, and the game wasn't as wary of Man as it is today. Gus told me how if you came upon a rabbit with a stick and you swung and missed, the rabbit wouldn't be so afraid that it would run so far you'd never see it again. But if you shot and missed with a gun, rarely would you get a second chance because the rabbit would hightail it into the next county. When a rabbit is startled, it will freeze momentarily.

One day Gus called me on the phone and said, "Ronald, I'm going to go cut a field"—what we call bushhogging. He said, "You want to come over and help me cut the grass? I've invited a few friends to hunt rabbits with us."

I said, "Sure, be right over," because when he asks for your help, you drop everything and give it to him. I don't care what you're doing. When Gus asks for help, you come running.

Ordinarily, Gus would sit on the tractor, and after the mower would cut down the cover, the rabbits would start hopping away, and I'd hunt them. On this day, I decided that I would drive the tractor so Gus could hunt. So I was sitting on the tractor driving, and Gus was sitting with me, and the other hunters were shooting at the rabbits as we flushed them out. I could hear the *boom, boom, boom* of the guns, but they weren't hitting any rabbits, and, boy, Gus was laughing at them. The hunters came closer, and they fired, *boom, boom, boom,* and missed, and Gus would just be doubled over. "Look at these guys," he said to me. "They have shotguns and they can't even hit a little rabbit."

The hunters saw Gus mocking them, and they were furious, I guess because they were embarrassed. Meanwhile, as I was sitting up on the tractor, I saw a rabbit come hopping out of the grass. I stopped the tractor and got down and took off my shoe. "What's he going to do? What does he expect to kill with his shoe?" they said to Gus. But Gus knew exactly what I was doing. He said, "You just hush up and watch." Sure enough, I walked to within a few feet of where that rabbit was standing there frozen and threw my shoe at it just as hard as I could. Hit the rabbit in the head and killed it instantly.

You should have seen the look on the faces of the other hunters. Gus, he just smiled. And I smiled back at him. The rabbit stew that evening was very enjoyable.

People also go alligator hunting in the bayous of Louisiana. It can be hazardous, but not as much as most people think if you know what you're doing. You can usually see them on the banks of the bayous or in the water. Of course, if you can't see them, you can't tell when they're around. Swampmen usually pass the word when they see a gator in the area, and everyone knows to stay clear.

Years ago, when my daddy's father was a little kid, a gator was sighted not far from his home. Several boys got ropes and captured the gator, which was about six feet long, and they dug a huge pit in the back of my great-grandfather's home, filled it with water, and put a fence around it. For years they fed it and made it a pet.

In 1927, the year my daddy was born, there was a terrible flash flood. The water rose about eight feet and the alligator was washed away. The hole, though, can still be seen. You can barely tell, because my great-grandfather used to raise sugarcane, and the refuse from the sugarcane filled the hole almost completely. But if you knew where to look, you could see that hole dug for the gator.

When Northerners think of alligators, they think of the old Johnny Weismuller movies. Scares them half to death. Recently several guys from *SPORT* magazine came down to see me, and they were paddling around the bayous while I was duck hunting. They paddled around a bend in the river, and there was a five-foot alligator sitting on a grassy knoll a few feet away. The cameraman in the front of the boat nearly tipped the boat over, he was falling over himself so badly trying to get to the back of the boat. In truth, alligators don't bother anyone—unless you bother them.

To hunt them, you use a sturdy fishing pole, heavy cord, and a big hook. You hang a piece of raw meat on the hook, dangle the meat out over the water, and go about your business. When the alligator surfaces, he'll take the bait and swallow the hook, and go under. After a while he'll have swallowed the hook so completely, he'll come right up when you pull up the rope. When you've got him up by the side of the boat, you shoot him behind the head. You have to be careful not to mess up the skin. It's now going for something like a hundred dollars a foot.

Frog hunting in the bayous is very exciting. Usually you hunt them at night, and it's best if three of you go—one to steer the boat, one to flash the light, and the third to catch the frog. The proper way to frog hunt is to quietly float down the bayou or canal, continuously flashing the light on and off. If you spot a frog, don't keep that light on, because too often it'll jump away. But if you flash it on him, then turn it off, he'll be stunned when he goes back into the sudden darkness and he'll freeze. If you're lucky enough, after a couple of flashes, you should be close enough to snatch it.

Ordinarily when frog hunting you grab the frog with a gig—which is a stick with a loop at the end—or you use your bare hands. Some people use a hook, but a hook will bruise the meat, so it isn't advised.

There is a certain amount of danger when frog hunting. When you flash your light and see two yellow eyes about the size of dimes, you know that's your frog. But here's where the danger comes in. One time Bobby Badeaux and I were out at night hunting frogs, and just as I was about to reach out and grab one, a cottonmouth, which is one of the most dangerous snakes in the United States, wrapped its fangs around it and pulled it under. It made me shudder. Another couple of seconds and the snake would have had the frog and me both.

Fortunately, a good trapper can smell a cottonmouth from twenty feet. They have a particular odor that is indescribable but unforgettable. As I said, if the eyes are about the size of dimes, it's a frog. If they're about the size of an eraser on the end of a pencil, that's a cottonmouth and it's hands off. If the lights are far apart, you hold back, because that's an alligator. If you see four lights, two on top of the other, you also pass that up. That's a frog riding on top of a gator.

There's one hunting experience I'll never forget. It was night, and Bobby and I were out behind my parents' home. We were walking through the woods and had just about come to a little bridge crossing a canal when we were suddenly face to face with a pair of eyes about three feet off the ground. We saw nothing else in the darkness, just the eyes. Bobby said, "It can't be a rabbit." I said, "Do you think it's a fox?" We said, "Let's go get Roland."

We ran back to the house to get my dad, and when we returned to the bridge the pair of eyes were still staring at us. Bobby had a flashlight and I had a gun, and so did my dad, and he and I surrounded it, moving carefully. Bobby and I watched my dad take aim, and we were waiting for him to shoot, but he never did. Instead we saw him slowly backpeddling, and Bobby and I looked at each other as if to say, "What the hell's going on here?" and just about that time we got a whiff of what it was. Unmistakably, it was a skunk. When we first got a whiff, everybody raced toward the house, but the night was cool and crisp and there was a north wind and we were downwind, and we got hit like we had run into a brick wall. The smell had enveloped us and the whole house by the time we got back there. My mother, Bonnie, and Bobbie's wife, Kathy, were inside and their eyes were watering when we came to the door. Everything smelled terribly of skunk, but what smelled worst of all was us. They made us take off all our clothes and leave them outside before we could come in.

I was also with Bobby the night we got our wits scared out of us. We got hungry for some rabbits, and I called my dad and said, "If Bobby and I should happen to get a couple rabbits, will you cook them?" He agreed. Hunting for rabbits at night with a flashlight is illegal, but when we get that urge to eat rabbit, we would throw caution to the wind.

We have a favorite spot to hunt them. There's a long, long road that becomes a trail through a field, and we'd drive very slowly down the path, shining the car headlights to spot the rabbits. We drove down this road to the end, shooting a couple of rabbits, and when we got to the end we turned around to see what we could shoot on the way back. We were creeping along as fast as the car would idle and move, two miles an hour, and at a certain point the road gets very narrow and trees branch over the road, and it's pitch black. Bobby was driving and I had the gun, and we spotted another rabbit. We were proceeding like turtles, and it was dark, and the night was cool and crisp so that a cricket's chirp was magnified into a loud screech. I pointed the gun, and from Bobby's side came a loud, *heeeeeeeeee haw heeeeeeeeee haw*. Bobby was so frightened he let go of the wheel and sank into his seat. I dropped into the seat and let my gun fall between my legs. My first reaction was, "We're caught." We were frozen in fear, afraid to see what had made that sound. Bobby looked outside his window, and there was a jackass eating grass alongside the road.

We had to get our breath back. We continued down the road and spotted another rabbit, but when I sighted my gun was shaking so badly I said, "That's it. Let's go home."

As much as anything else, hunting is a wholesome way to share experiences with friends, though sometimes those experiences can be filled with frustration. To understand fully what I mean you have to picture yourself crawling on your hands and knees for two hours in the damp, mud, and slush of a rice canal to get close enough to a goose to get a shot at it. You have to sneak up on a goose, it's the only way, and you have to do it very slowly and very carefully.

One time Bobby and another friend and I were driving around until we came to a field in the distance. Walking on that field were hundreds and hundreds of geese. A dyed-in-the-wool hunter will go to any length to come home with the goods, and there was no question in our mind that even though it would take us two hours or more to sneak up on those geese, it would be worthwhile, so down into the water-filled rice canal we went, beginning our crawl that would hopefully lead us to the geese.

It was cold and drizzling, perfect goose-hunting weather, and while we crawled inside that canal, we kept our heads down so the geese could not see us. We were within minutes of our destination, and we agreed that when we got to that point we would rise up over the bank and start firing, grab the dead geese, and hightail it home.

Quickly we popped our heads over the ridge of the canal, and just as we did so, another hunter, camouflaged in a burlap sack, rose up and started firing at the geese. He just started busting those geese . . . *pop, pop, pop, pop*. The geese were fighting each other trying to get up, and they were so close we could hear their wings knocking against each other as they tried to fly away. Geese were falling everywhere, and those that weren't hit took off. The hunter gathered up his catch and left, and as we watched him walk away we were standing in that damp canal very dejected. To crawl all that way and have another hunter make off with the prize!

I said to Bobby, "We're not going home empty-handed. Hold my gun. I'll be right back." Bobby didn't know what I was up to, but I had spotted a wounded goose hundreds of feet away wandering toward the canal. I ran down the canal to where I felt the goose would walk, and I waited. About ten minutes later, the goose wandered above me. I snatched it and ran with it all the way back. I showed Bobby the goose. "I told you I wasn't going to let us go home empty-handed," I said.

Another time when I was a little older my friend Richard Conques and I went hunting for geese. It was the middle of winter, and Richard had an old Volkswagen, the heater hardly worked on it, and we were riding around looking for a likely rice-field on which to hunt. It was getting to be about three in the afternoon, and after riding an hour or so we saw a big rice-field with thousands of geese on it. Now, as you might have guessed, hunting geese is hard work. As I said, you can't just walk up on them. You have to lay low and not let them see you.

We got out of the car with our guns, and there was a ten-foot-wide rice canal between us and the geese and then four hedgerows. There was a branch going across the canal, and Richard started shinnying across. The branch gave way and he fell into the canal and got soaking wet. He said to me, "You're not getting away with this. Get over here." I jumped and landed right into that canal and got soaked too. Were we miserable. But we kept crawling toward the geese. When we got close enough we fired our three shots, and I shot one. Just then, I heard a car horn, and when I turned around I saw a man standing next to his car parked beside Richard's. It was the man who owned the property. I said to Richard, "We've come too far not to come home with that goose."

He said, "You're right, pal."

I hid the goose behind me until I got within about fifty yards of the man's car, then I threw the goose into the bushes.

When we got to the car, the man said, "I heard you all shooting. What did you kill?"

We said, "Nothing, sir. We were too far off to hit anything."

He said, "You all know you're hunting on posted land."

I said, "I didn't see the signs, sir."

He said, "This land is posted. Any time you want to hunt, just come ask me." Then he drove off.

Richard said to me, "We're not leaving that goose here."

I said, "Right you are," and even though we were soaking wet and freezing our tails off, we were determined. "You're fast," he said. "Run into the brush and grab the goose, and I'll start the car, and when you get back here, we'll hightail it out of here." And that's what we did.

We got home when it was just about dark. I was living with my parents at the time, and when we got back, we found out that they had called the cops to find out where we were. They apparently thought we were coming back in the morning. Here it was five at night, and we were showing up. That's all we would have needed was a police car to pull up and catch us with that goose. Our own goose would have been cooked, but good.

Where I come from, hunting is a way of life. I'd be hard-pressed to name even a couple of guys who don't do it down here. For many people, it's a means of survival. When I was growing up, we always ate what we shot—duck, goose, rabbit, quail, whatever— because often there just wasn't much money to spend in the supermarket. I don't have that problem anymore, but I still eat everything I shoot, or I give it to friends who eat it. There's none of this killing for killing's sake.

Some people around the country don't understand how people can hunt, kill animals and birds. If you grew up down here, you'd see it differently. For generations my people have survived on their hunting skills, on their ability to master the wilderness. You grow up with it, it gets in your blood, and it's as important to your life as breathing. Hunting, fishing, and trapping have been the Cajuns' primary means of survival for hundreds of years, and you don't stop doing what your people have been doing for years just because suddenly you can afford to buy a hunk of meat in the supermarket. Someone had to kill that cow or chicken to get that meat into the supermarket.

People down here have a greater appreciation and understanding of wildlife than people anywhere else on earth. It's not a matter of taking your gun and shooting everything that moves. It's more of a science, of spending years in the wilderness studying, learning the habits of the animals and birds, and migratory patterns, and using that knowledge to your advantage.

I have never hunted indiscriminately. I don't go after endangered species. I don't use hunting dogs to find game. It's just me and them. One-on-one to see who can outsmart the other.

One fall afternoon I spotted a large red-tailed hawk. It was one of the most beautiful birds I'd ever seen, though I was only able to catch a quick glimpse of him before he saw me and flew away. I could see his red tail for quite a distance.

Just when I thought he was gone for good, he circled back, eyeing me cautiously, keeping his distance. Didn't trust me, I guess.

I was out again the next day, and the red-tail was there too. He had seen me before I saw him, and he stayed pretty far away. Almost every day that fall I saw him. He knew me, knew I was there, and he never did let me get too close.

I went on like this for about three years, and every time I saw him it made me glad. I'd wave, say hello quietly. Finally, he started to trust me. He'd swoop down and perch on a big limb of a cypress tree overhead, and even when I shot my gun, he'd sit there. That was a sign of trust, because hawks are very intelligent birds. They know about guns, and what they can do.

One day I saw him on a nearby limb, and he let me get real close. In a nest were two little adorable redtails. I thought to myself. "All along he is really a she." That was the last time I saw the red-tail. The afternoon she let me get close to her was her way of saying good-bye.

Even though I love hunting, I don't enjoy going after the bigger game, like moose and deer. When I'm shooting birds, I'm firing at tiny, darting specks overhead. With bigger game, there's an intimate, face-to-face contact.

Bobby and I were hunting one time in the Atchafalaya Swamp. It was early in the morning and we were hunting woodcock and had been walking a good ways in the woods. I sat down on a tree stump to catch my breath, and all of a sudden out from the bush came a big buck. How beautiful it was to see him in the wild! We were face to face, maybe fifteen yards apart, and I was looking at him and he was looking at me, and from the distance I could hear the bark of dogs that were tracking him.

As the sound of the dogs grew louder I started at him and said, "Hey, you better get going because they're coming closer." After a short pause, he started off through the bush, leaping fifteen feet in the air in a bound. After about a hundred yards, he stopped and looked back at me. Then he disappeared.

3

Once a Cajun, Always a Cajun

Mom and Dad are both Cajuns, and as far as I know that makes me the first Cajun ever to play in the major leagues.

The Cajuns originally came from northern France. They were Huguenots, French Protestants, who were kicked out by the Catholics in the 1600's. They sailed from France and settled in Nova Scotia in a region called Acadia, where they lived for 150 years, only to be kicked out again, again by the Protestants. In 1755, 8,000 Acadians were deported, crammed into ships and sent south. Longfellow's *Evangeline* is about the Acadian exodus. Half of them died before they reached their destination, which was the New Orleans area, chosen because of the French culture. Those who reached New Orleans settled in the southwestern part of Louisiana, in an eight parish area known as Acadiana with my hometown of Lafayette, the hub city. The term "Cajun" comes from the word Acadian.

Because of the hardship suffered by my people, Cajuns learned to be self-reliant. This self-reliance has been passed down from generation to generation, and as I look back at my childhood, I can see how my daddy passed it down to me.

When I was about four years old, two of my aunts came to visit. They wanted to go to a local nursery which was about ten miles from our house, and they didn't know the way. Mom and Dad were busy, but my dad volunteered my services.

My aunts couldn't believe a four-year-old could do it.

"Oh yeah, he can do it," he said. Daddy instructed me to take the old ladies to where Mommy and Daddy played bingo, which was right near the nursery. I knew how to get there. "Don't listen to whether he says left or right," Daddy instructed them. "Sometimes he gets mixed up. But if you watch the way he points, he'll get you there." I toddled into the car with the two aunts, and we had no trouble getting to the nursery and back.

Dad was always encouraging me to do things for myself. Once when I was about eight he took me fishing for the first time along with a couple of his friends. We were in a canal fishing for catfish. Daddy's friends told him they didn't think I should have come along. Daddy said, "We'll see." We sat in the boat awhile, and I felt a hard tug on my line. I began reeling in, and I was really struggling with that fish. My little muscles were straining, and I was using every bit of energy to keep from losing it.

One of the men started to reach for my pole. "Lemme give you a hand, son," he said.

My daddy screamed at him, "Get your hands off a there. It's his fish, and if he loses it, he loses it. But let him try himself."

"I sure do hate to see him lose that fish," the man said, which made me mad. I fought that fish even harder, and after about fifteen minutes of straining, I outlasted the fish and pulled it into the boat. It was a seven-pound shoepike, a big, strong fish. I had proved the man wrong, and I was darn proud of it. I turned to him and said, "I'm going to stop fishing now. I'll start again when you catch one bigger than mine."

The guy didn't know what to say, but a few minutes later he and the other friend began riding me, criticizing the fish I caught. They were saying things like, "Might as well throw it back. No use taking home a little thing like that." They kept this up until I had had enough.

"Look," I said, "when you catch one bigger, then you can say something. Otherwise keep your mouth shut."

The man told my father, "Your little boy has rude manners."

Daddy said, "No he don't. You do. You harass him and you keep harassing him, and he took everything you gave out. Now you take what he gives you."

The rest of the trip was quiet, and those two guys never did catch a fish as big as mine.

Cajun children are neither pampered nor tied down

by a blanket of rules and regulations. Parents show respect for their children, treat them like adults, and in my opinion the kids grow up more quickly this way and are able to stand on their own two feet at a very young age. This is not to say that parents do not feel deep concern at times. But they are often willing to listen to what their kids are trying to tell them.

My wife Bonnie and I treat our three-year-old daughter, Jamie, the same way. Outsiders are surprised at her independence and self-confidence. When we try to help her do something, she'll tell us, "I want to do it myself," and we let her. Ever since she was an infant, she's been crawling up and down the thirty or so steps from our first floor to the second. A lot of parents wouldn't have let her; it's amazing how many times I hear a parent tell their kid: "Don't do that. You might get hurt." But all this does is instill fear in the child and knock down any self-confidence a child might have. Sure, the child might get hurt once in a while if left alone, but that hurt doesn't compare to the hurt done to the child's way of thinking.

We don't hide anything from Jamie that we feel she should know. We don't do things behind her back, don't make her feel like an outsider. And unless there's a sound reason against it, we let her do pretty much as she pleases. If she wants to stay up until midnight, she does. Jamie knows when she's tired, and that's when she goes to bed—all by herself. My parents always treated me that way, and I appreciated it, and Jamie is treated the same way. There's no sense making a child do something she doesn't want to do, because that only brings resentment. Kids are very perceptive and sensitive, more than most adults think. After years of feeling restricted and sheltered, a kid will find a way to get back at you, to try and catch up on all that he missed during childhood. Cajun kids get to experience things when they're young. It makes for a greater stability when they get older. It also makes for a feeling of security, which again leads to self-confidence and a healthier outlook on life. But there are limitations, and when you exceed these boundaries you can expect quiet discipline. Hard, stern, but fair.

The Cajun lifestyle is unique. At least I've never seen anything quite like it. Ordinarily our lifestyle down here is very slow, smooth, and mellow. With patience and confidence, I *know* that everything will turn out the way I want it if I just wait. I never have to make a hasty decision, because I know that if I pass something up, it will come around again. I could let a bottle of beer age for fifty years before I drink it, that's how much patience I have. Up North, especially in New York City, the people are running all the time. Even when they walk, they run. Down here, you sit back and relax, and you don't miss anything. We do the same things people do in New York. We just do it more relaxed, because we know that in the end, we'll come out ahead. We have a special kind of contentment. Life is serene. There's no sense getting upset over things, because it doesn't do any good.

Gus taught me a lot about patience. One day he had a brand-new Chrysler, and I went to him and asked him if I could borrow it. When I returned, I noticed that the rear end of the car was making a lot of noise, and I was really upset. Here I had borrowed his new car, and I was bringing it back not working right.

I went in the house and told him, "Grandpapa, your rear end is going out."

But he said, "Don't let it bother you none. Don't worry about it. I'll get it fixed."

I got in the car to show him, and I backed it up, and Gus came over and said, "Ronald, there's a rock in the rear hubcap."

I said, "Grandpapa, don't be ridiculous. Your rear end is going."

He said, "Where's a screwdriver?" and he went and got one, pried off one of the back hubcaps, and sure enough, a rock fell out. He said, "Ronnie, you put the hubcap back on, get in the car, and drive it down the highway," and I did, and the noise went away.

Some other person might have gotten all upset and

angry because their car wasn't working right. Not Grandpa Gus. His attitude was, "Don't worry about it. If something's wrong with it, we'll get it fixed somehow." He never was one to let himself get all upset over something. He just figures, if it's going to happen, it's going to happen, and there's nothing you can do about it.

One time Gus was over his brother-in-law's cutting the grass, and the axle on the tractor broke. It didn't faze Gus at all. Gus slowly and calmly jacked up the tractor, and he fixed the axle, and before you knew it, he was back on that tractor cutting the grass again. No worry, no ulcers, no upset stomach. Gus figured, "If it takes me an hour to fix it, I'll do it. If it takes me five hours to fix it, I'll do it. No sense worrying about it." And then when he fixes it sooner rather than later, he's saved himself all that aggravation.

Because we're easy-going, however, doesn't mean that we aren't tough. When the Cajuns came to Louisiana, they had to use their wits and guile to stay alive. My great-grandfather was a rice and sugarcane farmer, and Gus was a farmer for a long time too. They had to go out into the woods to put food on the table. Cajuns are tough people. They take what's coming to them, and they'll work without a complaint. They will also do everything they can to avoid a fight, but heaven help you if you push them too far. We're like the Breaux Bridge crawfish we have down here. Back us into a corner where we can't be backed up any more and our claws come up.

My daddy is like that, and I am too. One night he was sitting in a local bar with one of my cousins, who was about six-foot-four and two hundred pounds. Now, Daddy isn't but five-foot-ten, and he probably doesn't weigh more than 165 pounds, but he's like me, he's stronger than he looks. He and my cousin were having a few drinks, and by midnight my cousin started getting a little too loud for his own good. Daddy said to him, "Son, I think it's time for you to be going home." Well, my cousin talked back. He said, "I'm not going and no one, not even you, is gonna make me."

Roland again said, "Son, you're going home, and now." My cousin, who never would have done this if he had been sober, got off the bar and put up his hands as though he wanted to fight.

Daddy said, "I hate to have to do this." Then he popped my cousin right on the jaw and knocked him cold. Daddy lifted him up, put him in the pickup, and drove him home, just like he said he would.

One time my momma and daddy were in a restaurant, and a man standing in a corner yelled over to Daddy real nasty, "Mister, come over here." My daddy said, "If you want to talk to me, you come over here." The man did, and he said to Daddy, "I don't like your face." Daddy said, "I'm sorry, but that's the only face I have. I don't like it either, but I have to live with it." Daddy didn't want any trouble. He was eating dinner. He wanted to be left alone. He said, "I can't do anything about my face." The other man said, "I can," and he took a swing at Dad. Dad bent over with his back to the man and let the man hit him, and when he straightened up, all hell broke loose. Dad pushed him over two tables and a bunch of chairs, and he backed the guy up forty to fifty feet, slapping his face the whole time. As he was slapping him, someone grabbed Dad from behind. It was a policeman, and the policeman had Dad's left arm in a bearhug. His right hand was free, and he reached back, got a hold of his neck, and flipped him over forward. He was flying through the air shouting he was a policeman. When he landed, Dad picked him up and said, "You should have come in front of me and let me see you."

In a Cajun fight, there's no such thing as a draw. It's either him or you. There's no tie in this ballgame.

I only got into one fight. In high school another guy and I were dating the same girl. After we both dated her, he asked her to go steady, and she accepted, which meant that it was hands off for me. As far as he was concerned, I couldn't see her, talk to her, or associate with her, which was impossible because we had a class together working on the yearbook.

On an earlier date with the girl I had left my tie at her house and there came a point when I had to have my tie back. I knew how jealous the guy was, but it was the only tie I had for a suit I wanted to wear and there was no way for me to get it if I didn't ask her for it. I called her and she told me, "You have to come over and get it." I wasn't too keen on doing that. I didn't want to incite the guy. No girl was worth fighting over. But I needed my tie, and I decided to go to the house where she was baby-sitting, get it from her, and go about my business. Except that just as I was leaving, her boyfriend drove up. I wasn't doing it on purpose, but obviously I was irritating the guy.

Several days later I was at a keg party and he was there. So was the girl. Everyone was there. I couldn't ignore the girl. I didn't want to seem rude, so when she asked me to get her a beer I did. After I brought it to her, he came over and we walked outside to have a little talk. "I don't think it's right your messing in," he said.

"All I did was bring her a beer," I protested.

The fight occurred not many days later. He was pushing for it, and he got it. It was a Friday night, and I was at Dave's Top Hat, a local hangout for teenagers. I was sitting in the back seat of a car with a couple of other girls from the yearbook staff when he and the girl drove up. I didn't think anything of it, but it wasn't long before one of his friends came over to me and said, "The man's in the back. He wants to talk to you."

I said, "Leave me alone. I came here to have fun. I'm not interested in any trouble. I have no reason to see him."

He said, "Guidry, why don't you just grow up," and he repeated it again.

I'm like a willow tree. I'll bend and bend and bend, but if I'm pushed too far, I'll snap. I said, "I'll show you how grown up I am," and I opened the car door and went to find him.

He hung around in a gang of about six rough guys, and I knew what type of guy he was. I had studied him, like I study the game when I hunt. I could almost read the guy's mind. I knew that he would lead me back where it was dark and try to sucker-punch me, what we call a sly lick. I was right. As I approached him in the back alley, I started shading over to the guy's left side so that when he turned to swing, I'd be on the other side of him. Which is what happened.

He spun to hit me, and when he did, I hit him with a ninety-mile-an-hour left. He fell. I picked him off the ground and stood him on his feet. He leaned against me, and I pushed him away and hit him again. He went down again, and that was the end of the fight. His face was cut and swollen, and after he went to the doctor, he had the nerve to send me the bill. I sent it back to him. I told him, "You asked for it, pal, and you got it."

Cajuns are mostly Catholic, and down here religion is important to us. As a child, I went to Mass just about every Sunday. Though I believe in God, I don't go to Mass as often as I should; but the Lord and I have private talks. I have a small prayer taped to my locker, and I recite it before I go out to pitch. If I'm in a hurry and don't have time to go over it, I'll say to Him, "I don't care if I win the game, I just want to be sure that I try as hard as I can."

Cajuns throw a lot of parties, and at family get-togethers there will be a father playing the accordion, and his son will play the guitar, and another relative will play spoons to make a clickety-clack, and maybe another guy will play the fiddle or the triangle, and they will play from nine in the morning until there's no more light. Cajun music is in French, and they'll sing in French, and then switch to English, or maybe sing one line in French and the next in English. It's great fun.

In Louisiana, Cajun festivals have become institutionalized. They're held all over the state. We have a shrimp festival, a crawfish festival, a dairy festival, and there are dozens more. A queen is chosen, and there's a parade, and out in the streets there's a big party with dancing in the streets. We don't need an excuse to have a good time.

The only time Cajuns rest is for forty days during the celebration of the Catholic tradition of Lent. But not before they have one last day of parties and enjoyment called Mardi Gras. Fat Tuesday. The day is so named to symbolize the tradition of having that one final day of eating, drinking, and pleasure before exercising stringent moderation during the forty days leading up to Easter Sunday. Then its back to the festivals.

During the 1978 season, we even had a Cajun festival in New York City.

Because sharing is so ingrained in the culture, a tremendous loyalty has been built up among the Cajuns. My people are proud that Ron Guidry made it to the majors, and I'm proud that they're proud.

John Schneider, my friend and attorney, was receiving repeated requests from friends and relatives for him to arrange a group trip to New York to see me pitch. So unbeknown to me, he puts together a weekend trip to the Big Apple for one hundred eager Cajuns. And he selects the weekend of my birthday and promotes it as Ragin' Cajun Weekend in New York.

The Adam's Apple on 2nd Avenue will never be the same. Forty of the more young at heart descended upon the establishment late one Saturday night and so overwhelmed the manager that he agreed to pick up the tip for the tab that ran into four figures. I have not figured out yet whether he did that because he was happy we were there or so happy that we were leaving.

The weekend was capped off with a surprise birthday party for me at the Sheraton Hotel near Hackensack, N.J. All my Yankee teammates were invited and many came. Catfish Hunter. Goose Gossage. Bucky Dent. Dick Tidrow. To name a few. Not only were they treated to a Cajun feast of crawfish étouffée, fried froglegs, fried catfish, and boiled shrimp, but they were all made Honorary Cajuns. They have the certificates to prove it. Which, if they are ever in South Louisiana and get a traffic ticket, they will get a strong cup of coffee and the sympathetic ear of a justice of the peace.

There are even some adopted Cajuns on the New York Yankees. Yogi Berra and Elston Howard are two of my favorites. Not only do I have to invite the two of them to share the rabbit stew my dad brings to Arlington every time we play Texas, but every four months I have to import from Louisiana gift packages of Trappey's pickled okra and hot sauce to keep them content.

Probably the most striking feature of the Cajun culture is the closeness of the Cajun family. I don't mean just Mom and Dad and the children. I mean aunts, uncles, grandparents, cousins, godparents. Historically, Cajun families have been very large, in part because we are Catholic, in part because in the days when living was hard, a lot of hands were needed to get the chores done. It's not like that today, but just a couple of generations ago, it wasn't anything special to have eleven or twelve kids. As I've already said, Grandpa Gus was one of thirteen. I heard of one Cajun couple who decided to name all their kids with the same initial. The names of the kids were Rita, Reus, Rayu, Rayance, Ray John, Regille, Raybe, Rhea, Raynard, and Ravide. When Daddy yelled for Ray, most everyone came running.

Ever since I can remember, we've been an extremely tight family. I was the only child until I was seventeen, and as I was growing up I remember how wonderful my parents were to me. Wherever Dad would go, I would follow along, and he was glad to have me. Now my mom was the disciplinarian in the family. I can't remember my dad ever giving me a licking. If I did something wrong, all my daddy had to do was sit me down, and he'd talk to me, and I'd listen and understand, and I'd have tears in my eyes when we were finished. I wouldn't do whatever I did again.

My mom gave me a spanking once. I was about four years old. I said something she didn't like, and she went to correct me, and I sassed her. She was telling me how it was for my own good, but I didn't want to hear it, I guess. I told her, "If you don't stop, I'm going to go to the park and drown myself."

She said, "If that's the way you feel, just go right ahead." She never expected me to walk out of the house, but I was stubborn. Very slowly I began walking toward the park, and every few yards, I'd turn around to see whether she was watching. Just as I was about to cross the road to go to the park, she appeared, and she wigwagged her fingers for me to come back. She ran up to me and caught me, and all the way back to the house she did not spare the rod. I was crying, and she was crying worse than I was. But the whole time she was hitting me I knew it was for my own good.

When I'm home during the off-season, hardly a day goes by that I don't see or talk to my parents and to my grandparents. In so many parts of the country, people act like its a chore to visit their relatives. Or else the family members live so far away from each other that it's impossible to visit often. That's a shame. It's just not like that where I'm from. It's tough to feel lonely in Cajun country.

During the baseball season I call my parents on the phone after every game I pitch. Not a long conversation. Just to say, "Hi. How you feeling?" to know everything is okay. They've always been behind me once my mom got over her fears of my getting hurt, and so have the rest of my relatives. I've got a ninety-eight-year-old great-great-aunt who follows my career as close as anybody.

I love pitching when my family's at the ballpark. A couple of years ago a whole bunch of family and friends drove up to Arlington, Texas, to watch me pitch. I really wanted to throw a great game for them. About the seventh inning, I was in a jam. A couple of runners were on base, and when I looked at our dugout, Bob Lemon, our manager, was coming out. He had that look in his eye like he was going to take me out, and by the time he reached the mount I was kind of worked up about it.

"No way I'm giving up the ball," I told him, holding the ball behind my back. "My grandfather's in the stands, my daddy, and I got a lot of friends who came all the way from Lafayette to watch me pitch, and you can't have the ball."

Lemon hadn't said a word. He looked puzzled. "Ronnie," he said, "I didn't come out here to take you out. I came to talk to you about how to pitch the fella in the batter's box."

"Oh," I replied.

I got the batter out, went the whole way, and won. It was a proud day.

The Cajun bond also extends to neighbors. This is also part of our culture, a trait handed down as a result of the rather simplistic way of life that has existed only until recently. To survive, we had to rely on family, friends, and neighbors. If my grandfather went out and shot ten ducks, he could only eat a few of them. There was no electricity, and no refrigerator, so to keep the rest of the ducks from spoiling, you gave them to family, friends, and neighbors. When a neighbor had extra ducks, he gave them to you.

Because we're so close, it's not surprising that strangers are regarded with a certain amount of suspicion at first. I remember my momma's Daddy used to say, "There are three kinds of people: Cajuns, Americans, and Yankees." The Yankees were from the North. Granddaddy'd say that Yankees could become Americans so long as they didn't try to con anybody.

Fortunately, that suspicion fades quickly. You can tell if you're in trouble if you come into a Cajun home and aren't offered a cup of our coffee. On the other hand, if you are offered a cup, don't dare refuse it. You don't have to drink it, but don't refuse it. It's the ultimate insult to a Cajun.

Cajuns are funny in that once you're accepted, you become like one of the family. My daddy says, "When

61

you come into my house the first time, I'm delighted to get you a beer and a sandwich. The next time you come, if you don't feed yourself, you ain't gonna get fed."

There are so many misunderstandings about us Cajuns. Some people think we're a tribe of Indians. Some think we're mysterious swamp people who migrate from bayou to bayou. Grandpa Gus told me he ran into someone in New York who thought a Cajun was a small, furry animal.

My daddy works as a trainman on the Amtrak run between Lafayette and Houston. A woman onboard knew him because she rode the train a lot, and one day she said to him, "All I keep hearing about down here is Cajuns. Who are these blasted Cajuns anyway? Where do they come from? Are they civilized? What do they look like? Would I know one if I saw one?"

My daddy smiled at her. "Ma'am," he said, "you've been looking at one."

4

A Hamburger, Cheeseburger Life

When I was sixteen, I started playing American Legion ball. In Lafayette there were two Legion teams. One year one team would be made up of the older boys, and the other would have the rejects and the kids coming up from the Colt League, and the next year they'd flip-flop. That way, one of the two sponsors, Shell or the Guaranty Bank, would have the better team every other year. It kept both sponsors interested.

My first year I played for the Guaranty Bank. The Shell coach picked all the best players, and our coach, Ray Boudreau, was given what was left over. Our local newspaper predicted that our team would win exactly two games.

I thought we had a hell of a team. Our Colt League team had gone to the state championships the year before, and even though we were young, I knew we had a good team. I couldn't understand why the papers put us down like they did. I said to myself, "If we can win only 2 or 3 games, then these other guys are professionals."

It took us about two weeks to show everybody what we could do. We beat the best team, and then we beat Shell, and we ended up second in the league by a game. That year I won 9 and lost only 1 game, and the team lost but 3.

In Legion ball I really progressed as a pitcher. I grew to my full height, though I didn't weigh much over 130 pounds, but I could really throw, and of course, I could really run. At my first practice coach Boudreau took one look at me and predicted that I'd get hurt. My first at-bat, I lined a bullet into right-center, flew around the bases, and pulled into third with a triple. A couple of innings later, I got to pitch, and I threw the ball past everyone. I made sure Boudreau knew who he was dealing with. I don't like people jumping to wrong conclusions about me.

Ray Boudreau, who was thin and left-handed and a pitcher himself, was a big help to me. He might have become a pro if he hadn't hurt his back. He taught me all he knew about pitching: how to pitch to a hitter, work the ball in and out, up and down instead of just throwing it up there, how to bend my back to take the stress off my arm, how to think. Ray was one of the first to realize the full extent of my potential. I was an American Legion star, but he made me look beyond Lafayette and Legion ball, made me realize that though I was good, there was so much more that I had to learn. "It won't always be this easy," he'd be telling me constantly. "Unless you use your head, the hitters are going to catch up to you, and you'll be in trouble."

Boudreau would harp at me constantly about being a thrower. "Ya got a long way to go yet, Ronnie," he'd say to me, even after I pitched a good game. Now when I see him, I'll say, "How'm I doing, coach? Am I a pitcher yet?" and we'll both laugh. I owe Ray Boudreau an awful lot.

Two games stick out during my three years of Legion ball. In the first one I came within one pitch of a perfect game. Funny, I can't remember the name of the team we played, but I do know that in this game Bobby Badeaux was playing the outfield. Usually he caught when I pitched. This game a fellow by the name of Jimmy Hernandez caught, and it was the last inning, and there were two outs, and not one runner had reached first. Not even one walk. There were two strikes, and I came in with a fastball that tailed away, and the batter swung and missed, but so did Hernandez. The batter started running to first, and Jimmy went after it, he still had a chance to throw him out, but he threw it over the first baseman's head ruining the perfect game. Before making another pitch, I picked him off first.

The other game I remember was against the top team in the league, New Iberia, where Tabasco sauce is made. Their pitcher was a guy named Al Dorsey, who was supposed to be a real hot-shot. New Iberia was the talk of the league, but again, when I saw that in the papers, my reaction was, "We'll see."

I pitched, and we won something like 25–3. In the

first inning we scored 10 runs. Badeaux made the first two outs. He was sitting there on the bench praying that we'd end the rally before he got up again. He didn't want to be responsible for all three outs. By the end of the game we got so tired of scoring that our coach told us to take chances, to get ourselves thrown out on the bases to get the game over with. We had a runner on second, and he walked halfway down to third, the pitcher stepped off the mound, threw to second, and threw it into center field. We had them so rattled they couldn't do anything right. When the ballgame was over, their fans were so angry we had to fight the crowd to get away from there.

There was no high school baseball where I grew up, so American Legion ball was my only avenue for advancement. This was during the mid-1960s when baseball was at a low ebb, and, Louisiana being a football-minded state, I was grateful for my opportunity.

It gives me great pleasure today to attend the Legion banquets and talk about my experiences. I'm also proud to say that Legion ball today is ten times bigger than it was when I was playing, and now that the high schools have teams, I'm hopeful that we'll be seeing more boys from the Lafayette area playing professional ball. Most important, more kids have a greater opportunity to participate, and to me that's the function of organized sports.

My next challenge was getting into college. I was a fair student, nothing to write home about, but my feeling was that if I didn't get a scholarship, I could go to work, and help support the family. My dad had only gotten through tenth grade, and yet there are few people whose intelligence I respect more. Dad had been a carpenter, a mechanic, he can fix most anything. He's a manager on the railroad, and he's even something of a tax expert. Until a few years ago he did my taxes every year, and he does a lot of other people's too, and he didn't need special classes to learn any of this. He decided it was something he wanted to do, and he did it, and I figured I'd be able to do the same thing.

66

Sometimes my momma would get on me about doing better. She'd say, "Ronnie, where are your books? Why don't you ever bring them home? Why aren't you studying?"

I'd tell her, "I did it all in school, Momma."

College to me was a chance to play more baseball. I'm not overly proud of that, but that's the truth.

I had set a couple records in track for Northside High (as I said, the school didn't have a baseball team), and in the spring of my senior year I received an offer for a track scholarship from Notre Dame. I turned it down. The first thing I thought was, "There's no money in track." I wanted to play baseball. I had heard that the local Lafayette College, the University of Southwestern Louisiana, was interested in giving me a baseball scholarship, which would have been fine with me. My only question was whether USL wanted me badly enough.

Before one of the Legion games, the director of the league, a gentleman by the name of Tigue Moore, told me that the USL athletic director was attending the game. "Make the most of it," Mr. Moore told me.

I struck out two of the first three batters, and in the second inning I struck out the side. I learned later that the coach, now USL's athletic director, Sonny Roy, had left after the second inning.

"Where you going?" Mr. Moore asked him.

"I've seen enough," Mr. Roy said. A week later I had my scholarship offer.

Because I lived at home, USL didn't have to pay my room and board. I learned later that coach Roy didn't know whether I'd make it as a college pitcher. He knew I'd done well in Legion ball. What he didn't know was whether I could cut it against stronger opposition. Had USL had to pay my room and board, it would have been less likely for me to have been offered that scholarship. And that very well may have affected my future in baseball.

The USL team started practicing in the fall of my freshman year. Our coach, Bob Banna, had inherited a weak baseball program. Baseball had been a stepchild to football. No one ever attended USL baseball games, so baseball was always costing the school money. Coach Banna was determined to change that. So when the final day of football was over, he started us running wind sprints. Rain, snow, or sleet, he had us out there, running sprints, running up and down the stadium steps, working out. And during this whole time I don't think he said one word to me.

In the spring, it was the same thing. He was concentrating on working with the experienced players, and I guess because I was still so skinny-looking, he never took notice of me. The season started, and I sat. After eight games into the season coach Banna became angry with some of the regulars. His goal was to stop the foolishness that losing had generated in the past. One day, to show his regulars a lesson, he put me in to pitch in a practice game. No one hit me. Still, coach Banna hadn't been impressed until one of the regulars went up to him and said, "Coach, that boy can throw that ball." At that point coach Banna thought back to the practice game, and he said, "You're right. I guess he can at that." After that game, coach Banna put me into the starting rotation, and I proved to him I could pitch college ball. I finished the year 6–1.

That year my brother Travis was born. I'll discuss him in greater detail later, but it's enough to say here that he was born retarded, costing my parents a lot of money for his medical care. I was tempted to drop out of college and get a job. I cut classes, and when I went I dreaded every minute, but coach Roy and coach Banna got on me to study, kept on me so I would be eligible to pitch again the next year. Scouts had given me a look toward the end of my freshman year, and so I decided to stick it out to play one more year of college ball and no more. If I could get an offer to play baseball, that money would come in handy in helping my parents take care of my baby brother.

The summer after my freshman year in college, our Legion team went to the state championships. Games were normally 7 innings, but it was 0–0 at the end of 7, so we had to go into extra innings. We won 1–0 in the twelfth, and I struck out 22. I've never felt more invincible. Unfortunately, there was a rule that you couldn't pitch more than 12 innings in three days, so coach Boudreau couldn't even use me in relief, and we lost the next two games and the championship.

At USL the next spring I was no longer an unknown. Coach Banna had faith in me, and when he needed to win a big game, he called on me, which gave me a great feeling. One game we traveled to Tulane, which at the time was the number-four-rated team in the country. We rode in a bus to New Orleans, and when we got there, we couldn't help noticing the new stadium with fancy lights, the marching band, cheerleaders, fitted uniforms of their players. They looked so professional, and here we were with our baggy flannel uniforms. We felt like orphans.

Coach Banna hadn't planned to pitch me that day. The next day was a conference game, and this wasn't, and he wanted to save me for the conference game, but his pride finally got the best of him, and just before the game he handed me the ball and said, "Ronnie, let's whip their ass."

I said, "Yes, sir, coach," and I pitched a 2-hit shut-out.

We played in a tournament, and as a result of the draw, we played against Louisiana State University, which had been avoiding us for the past two years. This was a Saturday, and again Banna had wanted me to pitch in a conference game the next Monday, but I wanted very badly to pitch against them, and coach Banna was good enough to let me. There were a lot of scouts in the stands for this tournament, and I was sky-high for facing LSU, and when I went out there I threw that ball as hard as I ever did in my whole life. I pitched 4 innings and allowed 3 hits. I struck out the first 9 batters. And it was at that point that I felt for the first time that a major league team was going to draft me.

I finished the year with a 7–4 record. The last day of the season I pitched a doubleheader against Nicholls State and lost both games. There were three teams in contention for the conference title, and we needed at least one win to get a tie. We were playing the second place team, and I pitched the first game, and we lost 1–0 on an error, and I told the coach, "This is too much for someone else to handle. Let me throw, because if I'm the goat, nobody's gonna say anything. I'd rather me lose the whole thing than go with someone else and wonder whether we were good enough." I thought that if I was the best pitcher on the staff, I should be the one to go out there. If I lost, I knew I could bounce back. I didn't know if the other guys could. So I started the second game, and the same guy who made an error in the first game made one in the second, and we lost 2–1. And I accepted it. I was never ashamed to lose, I knew we had done the best we could, and that was what was important.

The summer after my sophomore year Dodger scout Tony John arranged for me to pitch in Liberal, Kansas, for the Liberal Bee Jays. My manager was Bob Cerv, who used to be an outfielder for the Yankees. I finished with a 9–0 record against first-class competition, and in one game I defeated Burt Hooten, who was a highly rated prospect at the time. After I pitched the game to win the state championship, however, I hurt my pitching arm, tore some ligaments. I had experimented with a slider, and my arm hurt so much from throwing it I couldn't even pick the ball up. I'd cry it hurt so much, and I was scared I'd never be able to play again, and that I wouldn't get drafted by the pros.

I hung around the club until the end of the season, and when I returned home, coach Banna told me not to panic. He advised me not to touch a baseball until the spring season began. His advice proved sound. My arm was fine in the spring, and I never had trouble with it again.

I went back to school fall term, but it was getting more and more difficult for me to continue. I wasn't passing all of my courses, and coach Banna and one of the football coaches who served as the academic adviser brought me in for a meeting and chewed me out. They told me I was never going to make anything out of my life because I wasn't hitting the books, but I told them I had my heart set on playing professional baseball.

All the while Yankee scout Atley Donald was calling coach Banna, trying to find out whether I intended to stay in school, because if I dropped out before the spring semester, then I would be eligible for the June player draft. If I stayed in school, I wouldn't. Coach Banna passed this information on to me, and that made up my mind for me. If the Yankees wanted to draft me in June, then I wasn't staying in school. I wanted to play pro ball, and this was my chance. Mr. Donald told coach Banna they'd give me ten thousand to sign, and coach Banna knew how much money my folks were spending for Travis, and so he told me that if I dropped out and signed, I could always come back to school if things didn't work out. Coach Banna was putting my interests above his; and I'll always be grateful to him for that.

By the time the draft rolled around in June, I had been contacted by every major league organization but two—the Cincinnati Reds and the Yankees, from whom I didn't get a letter or a postcard, nothing. I was disappointed I hadn't heard from the Yankees, but I knew they were looking for players like Babe Ruth, Mickey Mantle, Yogi Berra, great stars, and I figured to myself, "What are they going to want with a peon like me?" I felt you had to be a superstar or God to play with that team.

The day of the draft was June 1, 1971. I knew I could go high, but I didn't know where or when. Mom and I were sitting home watching television, and they announced the first round picks, and then they announced the second round picks, and as we were sitting there quietly, the announcer came on again and said, "Lafayette native Ron Guidry was picked by the New

71

York Yankees in the third round." I heard this, but I didn't react. No screaming. No hollering. Silence. I looked at Mom and she looked at me, and we were both shaking our heads. It didn't register that they're talking about me. There were about ten Ron Guidry's in the Lafayette area, but this one here was the only one who played baseball. While we sat there dumbfounded, the phone rang.

I picked it up. There was a long distance call from Atley Donald, the Yankee scout. He asked whether he could come over and see me the next day, and I said of course, and we hung up. Mom said, "Who was that?"

I said, "Atley Donald of the Yankees. I was drafted third."

At that point I started shouting. I ran around the kitchen like a crazy person, and then I started calling around. I called Grandpa Gus. I called Dad at the railroad station to see whether he was on the tracks or on the road. He was on his way to Houston. I sent him a message. And then the phone started ringing off the wall.

What I didn't know at the time was that Atley Donald was the only scout who was aware that I was eligible. He had been in touch with coach Banna, unlike the rest of them, and he knew I had dropped out of school when everyone else still thought I was ineligible for the draft. The Yankees offered me ten thousand dollars to sign, plus incentive bonuses of $7,500. I was told later that the Dodgers were prepared to offer me a lot more money to sign, but on the day Atley Donald walked in the door anything over a hundred bucks was a lot of money to me, so I was glad to sign. When he said that he wanted to give me money to play baseball, I was looking all over the room. I couldn't believe it was happening to me. Mr. Donald left the contract with me. I told him to call in a couple of days, that I wasn't going anywhere.

When my dad came home, I talked it over with him and my mom. Dad said, "Remember the time you wanted a glove and you suckered me into buying you one for fifteen dollars." We both laughed. He said, "You've proved to me that you can do whatever you want to do. Whatever you decide, I'll back you."

Mom said, "I don't really know about this. You're going to go away from home. Are you sure you're going to like that?"

I said, "Mom, I can't live at home forever."

5

No Way to
Treat a Guy

I played five years of minor league baseball before I got my chance with the Yankees. Maybe if I had signed with another club, I would have gotten my chance sooner. On the other hand, maybe if I were with another club, my major league record wouldn't have been so outstanding.

Looking back at my career, what I marvel at is that I made it to the major leagues at all.

I started at Johnson City, Tennessee, playing in the Rookie League in 1971. The first night I was there our team was involved in a beanball war. Terry Whitfield, who was a teammate and the Yankees' first draft choice that year, was hit on the shoulder with a pitch. The next inning our pitcher threw at one of their players. The umps called time and warned both benches to cut it out. When Whitfield came up the next time, he was hit in the head, fell unconscious, and suffered a concussion. A couple of innings later one of our players singled and headed for second trying to stretch it. Their second baseman covered and our runner bowled him flat. Their shortstop ran over and started punching our guy, and suddenly the benches emptied, the bullpens emptied, and both teams stood out there for fifteen minutes throwing punches and trying to do some hurt. It was a memorable way to start a career.

The next night I got to pitch, and quickly I found out that the guys in this league weren't even as good as the ones I had faced in college and in semipro ball. I appeared in seven games, had a 2–2 record with a 2.11 earned-run average, and I struck out 61 batters in 47 innings. I enjoyed the ballgames, but Johnson City was, in a word, dull. It didn't have anything to do. We'd sit around staring at each other, maybe go to the movies once in a while. Plus it was a dry town. We had to travel across the border into Virginia to get a drink.

The one thing I remember about Johnson City is that I opened a bank account there, and I haven't closed it yet. I didn't know whether I would be going back, so I left a dollar in it so I wouldn't have to go to the trouble of opening another account. Fortunately, the dollar is still there.

The next season I moved up to Single-A ball at Fort Lauderdale. Fort Lauderdale was a boom town, and it's on the ocean, and we would go scuba diving and swimming and drive down to Key West. The town was fun, but playing wasn't, because our team was so mediocre. We got kicked around every place we played. Personally, I was satisfied with my progress because I struck out a lot of guys, even though my record was only 2–4 with a 3.82 ERA. I came within one out of throwing a no-hitter. Even though I had walked 8 batters, no one had gotten a hit off me through eight innings. With two outs in the ninth and a man on first, the batter hit the first pitch right down the line just barely foul. Our third baseman was Steve Lindsay, who had one of the strongest arms in the league, and before the next pitch manager Pete Ward ordered Lindsay to back up and play the line to guard against a double. I threw, and the batter dribbled a twentyhopper down the third-base line, and he beat it out because Steve was playing so far back. As it was, it was a close play. If Steve had stayed put, he would have been out by five steps.

I had planned on marrying Bonnie during the season, but I was taking weekends once a month during the season for National Guard drill, and the Yankees refused to give me a couple more days for the wedding. It was April, and Bonnie had picked out her dress, and on the weekend I was home for drill, I gave her the bad news. She cried and cried. I told her, "They employ me. They don't want me to. We can't." We had to wait until the end of the season. We didn't have any money, and as it was for the first three years of our marriage, during the off-season we lived with my folks. Dad built us a room in what had been the carport, and we lived there.

My next step up the ladder, the first one I spent with Bonnie, was in Kinston, North Carolina. I was making about $150 a week, and when we got there, we couldn't find a place to stay. Kinston is a tiny town filled with elderly people, and there wasn't even a McDonald's or a Burger King. Nothing. No place—well, there was one place. It was a fast-food hamburger joint. I won't mention its name. But the first time we ate there we found dead flies in the hamburgers.

We found out that all the Kinston ballplayers were staying at a particular trailer park. We were one of the first to arrive, and we figured we had the pick of the trailers. We chose what looked to be the nicest and cleanest trailer. But when Bonnie opened the oven a mouse ran out. Our neighbors, Ray and Sharon Hall, had a whole nest of mice in their oven. And every time the wind blew I had visions of *The Wizard of Oz*. I figured the trailer would be lifted away to Kansas. Actually, that was what I was hoping. The walls and the roof would shake, and Bonnie and I would lie there wondering whether the trailer would survive the night.

The most fun I had in Kinston was driving around town in my GT-37 with the big glasspipe mufflers. The old ladies could hear me coming down the street from a mile away.

For Bonnie and the other wives, boredom was the biggest problem. My mom and dad and Bonnie's mom and dad got together and bought us a color TV set for a wedding gift, and Bonnie spent a great deal of time watching it. We went on the road for five days at a time, and it was brutal for her because there was nothing to do, no movie theater, no place to shop, no nothing.

In the middle of the season I had two weeks of National Guard duty, and when I returned, we went back to the trailer park. When we drove up to place where we had stayed, there was nothing but grass. The guy who ran the trailer park told us they had to move it and that they'd get us a new one, but the new one never came, and we spent the rest of the year sharing a trailer with another teammate, his wife, and their infant.

I kept having nightmares at Kinston. In one of them a huge baseball came down out of the sky, snatched me out of bed and carried me away. Another one I kept having, and I continued to have this one for a couple of years, was going into my windup, rearing back, making the big kick, and on my follow-through having my left arm fly right off my body and go spinning into space.

The worst one of all, though, was the nightmare of getting lost in the woods. I'd be wandering around, trying to find my way back, and all of a sudden a pack of hillbillies would come along and take me prisoner. Then, after we'd walk back to their little rundown mountain shacks, they'd use me as bait to catch wild animals.

Though it wasn't much fun off the field, on it I continued to pitch well. I won 7 games with a 3.21 earned-run average, and I struck out 101 batters in 97 innings, statistics that ordinarily make a front office executive sit up and take notice. Up I went, the next year to Double-A ball and West Haven, Connecticut, which for us was as bad, or even worse, than Kinston. West Haven always seemed so dark and gloomy, and on my $650 salary, we were forced to share our apartment again. We were living in a high-rise apartment, and it cost us $233 a month plus thirty dollars a month for parking, and after taxes were taken out of my paycheck, we didn't have much left over. We couldn't even afford to rent furniture, so we went to the Salvation Army and bought a mattress for ten dollars, and that was the only furniture we had. You can picture our apartment: a big color television set and a mattress.

After a night game, our roommate, Rob Arnold, said that back home in Pennsylvania he had a card table, four chairs, and a bunk bed that we could use, and so at midnight we drove to his home and brought back the goods.

In addition, we bought two plastic inflatable chairs which broke the first time we sat on them. That summer Bobby Badeaux and Kathy, who were now married, came to visit us, and all four of us slept in the same bedroom. They slept in their sleeping bag, and we slept on our Salvation Army mattress, while Rob Arnold in the next room slept on his cot. While they were there, we had the opportunity to eat out at the ballpark. It was ten-cent hot-dog night. We purchased forty hot dogs for the four of us and proceeded to eat them all as we drove to New York City after the game to show Bobby and Kathy the bright lights of Broadway.

On the field, West Haven was a disaster. I had been a starting pitcher since I was a kid, and in spring training Cloyd Boyer, a Yankee pitching coach, suggested that I move to the bullpen. "There's a lot of young guys who want to be starters," he said. "But somebody's got to be in the bullpen, and you'll probably have a better chance making the Yankees that way than as a starter."

I said, "Whatever you want you to do is fine with me so long as I pitch."

Boyer said, "Give relieving a try. If you don't like it, you can always go back." I agreed. What I didn't realize at the time, and what nobody, including Mr. Boyer, ever told me was that a pitcher must approach relief pitching in a different way than starting. When you're a starter, you can afford to make a mistake and still get out of the jam. As a reliever, you're coming in in a jam, and one bad pitch can lose the ballgame. The thinking is different, and the pitches you throw are different. As a starter you can mix junk in with your fastball to try to keep the batter off-stride. In relief, there's no margin for error. Every pitch has to be an "out" pitch, which better be good, because the batter knows it's coming and he's waiting for it. In Double-A the batters waited for my fastball, and they hit it, hard and often.

In 29 appearances I had exactly 3 saves. My ERA was 5.26, demoralizing numbers. Fortunately, I still struck out 79 batters in 77 innings, so the Yankees didn't give up on me.

Few people know this, but we were almost the late West Haven Yankees. We had just finished playing in Three Rivers, which is in Quebec, Canada, and our bus was bombing down the road when unexpectedly all the lights in the bus went off, including the headlights, and the engine went dead. We rolled for a couple of hundred feet before we stopped. The road was unlit, there were no other cars, and we could smell the pungent odor of burning wires. "Must have been a short circuit of some kind," said the driver.

Since I was the only one who spoke French, I went to the nearest house and rang the bell. The porch light was on, but when I knocked, it went off. I ran back to the bus.

The driver and I then flagged down a car. We got a ride to the police station, called the bus depot to find out no other buses were available, and so I called a taxi company and sent eight cabs to pick up the rest of the guys. We spent another night at our hotel.

The next morning we got a new bus, and as we were cruising along we passed our stranded bus. What we saw was that a couple of feet from where the bus had rolled to a stop in the dark, the road bent ninety degrees, and had it continued to roll straight, it would have plunged several hundred feet off a cliff into the St. Lawrence River.

My fourth year of professional ball was spent in Triple-A in Syracuse, one level down from the major leagues. I liked Syracuse about as much as Fort Lauderdale. It had been two years since I had been to a good town like that, and when we got there, we really enjoyed the atmosphere, the people, and being so close to New York City, which was an added incentive. I probably played harder at Syracuse than I ever had before. All I did at Syracuse was relieve. I started slowly, but by the second month I was tearing up the league. I figured my chances of making the Yankees were slimmer than none, because every time they needed a player they'd make a trade for an established player, but I wasn't discouraged because I was winning and doing a hell of a job. I was getting to know what I had to do to become a reliever, and I'd come in with the bases loaded and nobody out, and I'd strike out 3 batters. It was so rewarding, with teammates running out of the dugout and jumping all over me like it was the World Series. For the first time I got to feel that I was an important member of the team.

In late July our manager, Bobby Cox, called me over. "Ronnie," he said, "they want you in New York. Get on the first flight out of here, because they want you right away."

I arrived in New York. The Yankees were playing the Red Sox, and I went over to Shea Stadium to get the feel of what it was like being in the major leagues, and I was doing wind sprints in the outfield. I couldn't help thinking of how when I was eight or nine years old I would watch the Yankees on TV with my momma and I'd tell her how someday I would be pitching for the Yankees. I shook my head. Here I was pitching for the Yankees. Hard to believe.

It was late in the game, and Yankee manager Bill Virdon called down to the bullpen for me to warm up. An inning later I was in the game. Everything was happening so quickly I didn't have time to be nervous. I felt composed. In fact, I wasn't really conscious of being anywhere but on a pitching rubber in a baseball game. It was also when I met Thurman Munson. As I strolled in from the bullpen, Thurman met me on the mound. He said softly, "Don't get nervous. Just throw strikes." Then he surprised me when he asked me what my pitches are. Here I was in the major leagues before thousands of people, and the pitcher and catcher had never been introduced, much less one know what the other throws. I told him I threw a slider and a fastball. "OK," he said, "one's a fastball and two's a slider," and for three innings all I saw was one finger. I threw just as hard as I could, and in three innings I held the Sox scoreless and struck out three.

The next day Virdon called on me again, and this time it finally dawned on me where I was. I was more nervous than I had a right to be, and I walked the first two batters, and Virdon took me out. After that, I sat. The other guys were pitching well, and I wasn't needed.

I was working behind Sparky Lyle and Dick Tidrow. I was the third guy on a two-man bullpen staff.

Virdon was fired on Old Timer's Day, and Billy Martin replaced him, and everyone on the club felt optimistic that Billy would fire us up, and sure enough, we started playing better. The Red Sox, however, pulled away from everybody, and I pitched a few more times and figured that I would have a hell of a year for the Yankees in 1976.

To get a head start, I agreed to pitch winter ball in Venezuela. The Yankees wanted me down there for the entire three-month season, but I didn't want to go, and I only agreed when they said I'd only have to go for the first six weeks. That was long enough. I swear the people in Venezuela are crazy.

Before we arrived, the team was on a road trip and the wives had stayed behind, and while the wives were eating in a restaurant, a man came in and pulled a knife on one of them, a blonde. He was jabbering Spanish at her, and she was American and didn't know what was going on, and the other wives started hollering, and none of the men in the restaurant were making a move to help her. When the guys came back from their road trip, the wives told them about this guy; the day before we arrived, they found him lurking around their hotel and had him arrested. When I heard this, I said to myself, "Great, Bonnie's a blonde, I'm gonna feel really safe leaving her alone."

After that incident, a guard from the militia was assigned as the team's personal bodyguard. He had a machine gun, and his orders were to shoot first and question later, and he'd walk us to and from the ballpark, and he'd sit with the wives at the game, and at the hotel he was always there. I swear he never slept. Wherever we'd go, he'd be there too.

On New Year's Eve, Larvell Blanks, an outfielder for the Atlanta Braves, was playing Frisbee with his son, and somehow the Frisbee ended up on the roof of the hotel. It was a low, flat roof, so Larvell lifted the boy up, and he went and got it. The hotel manager, meanwhile, went berserk. He came sprinting toward Larvell, yelling at him in Spanish, I assume because the boy was on the roof. Larvell spoke Spanish, so he started yelling back, and all of a sudden a man with a gigantic machete came running over and started menacing a couple of our players, banging it against the wooden blinds and scaring hell out of everybody. Finally Bobby Cox ran over and apologized like crazy to the hotel manager, and everyone calmed down.

It seemed like incidents like that happened all the time. Once we were sitting around the hotel pool in early evening when suddenly we heard a shriek from one of our rooms. Vic Correll's wife was putting his little kids to bed when a man burst in on her. When she screamed, we went running up to the room, and the guy started apologizing, saying he was in the wrong room, that it was a mistake. Vic told him not to let it happen again, and he left, and we thought that was the end of it until our guard caught him trying to break into another room. Next thing I knew, a group of policemen with machine guns were chasing this guy through the hotel. When he was captured, Vic and Kenny Clay went to the police station to testify against him. In the station, Vic found out that the man was an escaped convict. After they talked to the cops, they took maybe three steps out the door and they heard gunshots. We heard three shots and assumed the man was killed on the spot.

We weren't even safe at the ballpark. During one game Nate Colbert's wife was sitting in the stands yelling for him to hit a home run, and a man in the stands who I guess was rooting for the other team, said something to her, and she said something back, and he spit into her little boy's hair. She had a knife in her purse, and she pulled it out, and the guy started fighting with her, and then Nate left the batter's box and ran into the stands, followed by the rest of the players in the dugout. Meanwhile, as the players and some fans were fighting, other people in the stands emptied their beer cups, peed into them, and tossed the cups at the people who were fighting. Six weeks of winter ball was enough for a lifetime.

When I got to spring training in '76 all the talk was that it was going to be Sparky Lyle and Ron Guidry out of the bullpen from the left side and Dick Tidrow from the right side. I was jubilant. At Syracuse in '75 I had struck out 76 batters in 62 innings, I had worked hard during spring training, didn't pitch badly, and I felt I was finally ready. I figured that Lyle and Tidrow would pitch short relief, and I would pitch in situations when they needed a reliever early in the game.

The only unsettling fact of life was that the Yankees had an awful lot of high-priced pitchers in camp. That winter Doc Medich was traded to the Pirates for pitchers Dock Ellis and lefthander Ken Brett (along with Willie Randolph), and another experienced lefty, Larry Gura, was added to the roster, and when I looked over our pitchers and saw that almost every one of them was making sixty, seventy thousand, I said to myself, "Big guy, you realize they don't have room for you?"

The day we were to break camp and fly to New York, Bonnie and I were talking about how exciting it was to be starting the season with the big club. My bags were packed, and I was sky high. Billy had told me the Yankees were about to make a deal with Texas and that I'd be on the club, so it was totally unexpected when Billy came over just as the rest of the players were getting on the bus to go to the airport. Billy looked pained. "Ronnie," he said, "I'm in an awfully tough spot. I can't send Gura down. I can't send Tidrow down. I can't send Brett down, and somebody has to go." He had mentioned every bullpen pitcher we had except Sparky Lyle and me, and I knew Sparky wasn't going anywhere. "You're going to have to be the one," he said. I was distraught, but he did leave me some hope. "We're still working on that trade, and you ought

85

to be back up here shortly. Go down and pitch like you had been, and we'll take care of the rest." I told him okay, but when I told Bonnie, she cried her eyes out. She was pregnant and wasn't feeling good, and we were both angry and very upset with them for raising our hopes and then dashing them—for waiting until the last minute to let us know.

We took a couple of days off, went down to the Syracuse minor league camp, and then we stopped at Disney World on our drive back to Syracuse.

When I got back to Syracuse, I picked up right where I had left off. I went through the league like a knife going through soft bread. The first month I pitched 22 innings, gave up something like 6 hits and 2 walks, and struck out 27.

It was mid-May, and I was playing in Rochester, when the Syracuse owner called me to tell me the Yankees wanted me to rent a car and drive to Syracuse and then fly down to New York. The Yankees had traded Gura and Brett and were bringing me up as Billy promised. I got back home at about one in the afternoon and had to make a three-o'clock flight, and here I was leaving Bonnie all alone to pack all our stuff to bring to New York. Bonnie and a couple of the Syracuse ballplayers moved everything out of our apartment into our car, and she drove to New York, where we kept all our things in a hotel for three weeks until we were able to find an apartment.

We found an apartment in Fair Lawn, paid the $375 security deposit, and settled in. Meanwhile, I pitched four days in a row for Syracuse before I was recalled by the Yankees. My arm was dragging, and when I reported I went into Billy's office and told him not to use me for a couple days.

The day I arrived the Yankees were playing the Red Sox, and it was about the fifth inning, and I was sitting out in the bullpen enjoying myself when the bullpen phone rang. Billy was calling down for me to warm up. "Damn," I said. "I told him my arm was tired."

There were two runners on base and nobody out when I came in. When I left there was one out and no runners on base. I had given up two singles, a triple, and a home run.

It was the last time I pitched that summer. Apparently Billy didn't trust me after that. We were in the middle of a pennant drive and were leading the league, so he went with his veterans. I sat, didn't say a word. What could I have said, "You gotta pitch me"? So I said to myself, "Be patient and you'll get your chance." I went to the ballpark, shagged flies in the outfield, dressed and undressed, and sat. The whole time Billy didn't say one word to me. I felt like a ghost.

Meanwhile, all I kept reading in the papers was that I was going to be traded. The first time I read this I was with Syracuse, and we were playing Richmond, and I opened up the paper, and it said: Cowens-Guidry Deal Off. The Yankees were going to trade me to Kansas City, but the day before the trade was to be made, Royal centerfielder Amos Otis got hurt, and Kansas City called it off. I must admit that I was stunned when I saw my name in the headlines. I must also admit that at the time I was disappointed the trade wasn't made, because I felt it would have been my ticket to the big leagues.

Another trade I was almost involved in was between the Yankees and Baltimore. We traded Scott MacGregor, Rick Dempsey, Rudy May, Dave Pagan, and Tippy Martinez for Kenny Holtzman, Doyle Alexander, and Grant Jackson. The Orioles wanted me rather than Tippy, but Gabe Paul wouldn't budge, and the deal was finally completed without me just before the June 15 trading deadline.

On the forty-sixth day after that disastrous Boston game, general manager Gabe Paul called me into his office. I couldn't imagine what he wanted.

"Ron," he said, "we're sending you back to Syracuse."

"Why?" I almost shouted at him.

"Because you're not pitching," he said.

"Well, why don't you give me a chance to pitch?" I asked.

"That's exactly what I'm going to do," he said. "At Syracuse."

I stormed out of the office, drove home in a blind rage, and when I arrived back at our apartment, I sat down and had a heart-to-heart with Bonnie.

I told her about Syracuse, and I said, "We have to be realistic. I'm twenty-six years old and I've spent five years in the minor leagues, and now I'm going back. My time is too valuable to be wasting like this, and I'm not going to put up with people treating me like this. We will never make a decent living unless I find another field. If this is all they think of me, then let's forget it. Let's go back to Louisiana and forget about this." I was serious, but before I left I decided to talk with Yankee owner George Steinbrenner about how I was being treated. I called his office, and his secretary said he wasn't in. The next day I called his office, and his secretary told me he wasn't in. The next day my demotion to Syracuse was official. I called Steinbrenner again. He still didn't return my call.

We packed our belongings in the car, and I was headed home. No two ways about it. I was through. Route 80 is a six-lane highway extending from the George Washington Bridge west. How far it goes, I'm not sure, but it goes far enough to get me on the right road to Louisiana. I drove, and for more than an hour we headed west through New Jersey without saying a word to each other. A great rage had built up inside me, and I was unable to make small talk. I hadn't told Bonnie we definitely weren't going to Syracuse. At the end of the hour of riding I was able to tell her.

Bonnie said, "Where are we going to go?"

"Back to Lafayette," I said quietly.

"What are you going to do when we get there?" she said.

"I'll find something to do."

Toddler Ron and his dog

His first wheels

Ron age 2 years, 4 months

Southern Bell Half-pints,
Ron's first ball club

High School Yearbook photo

Shell Royals Colt League team circa, 1966. Ron, second from left, middle row—Bobby Bordeaux, far left, bottom row

Pitching for the University of South Western Louisiana, 1969

Mom, Dad, Ron, and Travis, 1970

Ron and Travis, 1972, the year he was pitching for Fort Lauderdale in the minors

Ron, Travis, Bonnie, and a mound of crawfish

The whole family: (from left) Randy Matthews (Bonnie's brother);
Joyce Matthews (Bonnie's Mom); Russell Matthews (Bonnie's
Dad); Jamie Guidry; Bonnie Guidry; Ron Guidry; Travis Guidry;
Roland Guidry; Grace Guidry; Grandma Gladys Guidry; Grandad
Gus Guidry (Photo by Philip Gould)

Opposite Page Bottom: Ron and his dog, Lightning, behind his
home (Photo by Philip Gould)

Family dinner at the Guidry's (Photo by Philip Gould)

Opposite Page: Ron and daughter, Jamie (Photo by Philip Gould)

(Photos by Philip Gould)

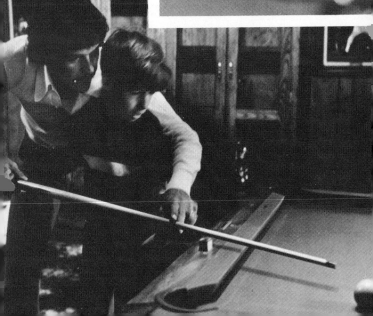

From left: Gus, Ron, Roland and Rus Matthews (Photo by Philip Gould)

Bonnie, Ronnie and Jamie before they could afford their own home (Photo by UPI)

Opposite Page: Recent photo of Ron and Travis (Photo by Philip Gould)

September 1977, Yankees mob Guidry after he defeats the Red Sox 4-2 (Photo by UPI)

Opposite Page: At work (Photo by the New York Times)

Following pages: (Photos by John Woodward)

October 1977, Ron defeats Kansas City to tie American League Play-off at one game each. Thurman Munson, Cliff Johnson, Chris Chambliss, and Graig Nettles join in the congratulations (Photo by UPI)

September 1978, Guidry two-hits Cleveland for twenty-third win (Photo by UPI)

Signing autographs in San Diego (Photo by UPI)

October 1978, walking off after pitching 6 1/3 innings against the Red Sox in the Play-off game. It was Guidry's 25th win of the season (Photo by UPI)

Relaxing in Yankee locker room in the midst of the Pennant race with Boston in 1978 season (Photo by UPI)

In an unusual effort to help the team, Ron goes in as a relief pitcher for Catfish Hunter in the Spring of 1979 (Photo by John Woodward)

Facing the Press
(Photo by UPI)

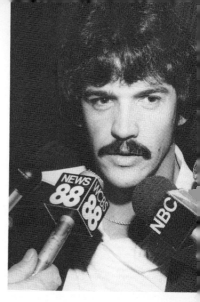

Thurman and Ronnie
(Photo by UPI)

Photo by Philip Gould)

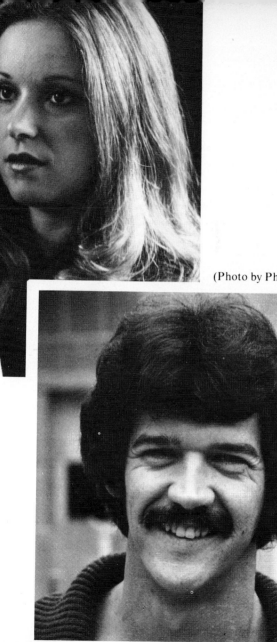

(Photo by Philip Gould)

(Photo by Philip Gould)

Bonnie said, "Ronnie, you've never worked a day in your whole life. All you've ever done is play baseball, and you wouldn't be happy doing anything else."

I pulled the car over to the side of the highway and turned off the engine, and I recounted to Bonnie how I had been treated by Billy and Gabe Paul and Steinbrenner. "You can't let people treat you that way," I said.

Bonnie said, "You've never quit like this. It's the first time I've seen you walk away from something before you knew for sure whether you could master it or not. You know you can play major league baseball. When the time comes that *you* decide you can't, that's the time to go home. Not now. Don't let them destroy your ego the way they've been doing. You have to fight them."

I said to Bonnie, "You're the one who has to do all the packing and moving. If you don't mind, then we'll go to Syracuse."

She said, "It's kind of routine to me now. I've done it so many times, I don't mind. I'm game. Let's give it one more shot."

"Okay," I said. "One more shot. But if it doesn't work out, that'll be it."

I restarted the engine, checked my map, and after driving through some Pennsylvania back roads, we headed north on Interstate 81 for Syracuse. To this day I'm not sure the Yankees know how close they were to losing me.

Back at Syracuse I once more felt invincible. In my first game back Syracuse manager Bobby Cox sent me in in the eighth inning with the bases loaded and nobody out. It had been a long time since I was in a game, but I was ready. My adrenaline was flowing, and when I stood out there, I felt ten feet tall. I struck out the side on ten pitches and struck out two more in the ninth. When I got the final out, my teammates poured out of the dugout. It felt so good to be appreciated again.

I pitched for Syracuse exactly one month. When we got back to Syracuse, we rented a one-room efficiency. After a couple weeks, I returned from a long road trip. It was about eleven o'clock in the morning when Syracuse owner Tex Simone called. Bonnie answered. Tex said, "I'm sorry, Bonnie, but . . ." Bonnie knew exactly what he was going to say, that I was going back to New York and the Yankees. Bonnie just started crying. She hardly ever cried in front of me, but inside she was feeling, "Not again," and she couldn't help it.

Outside the weather was getting bad. It was dark, cloudy, and gloomy, and Bonnie drove me to the airport, and at the airport here was Bonnie big and pregnant and crying her eyes out, and here I was leaving her behind, and all these people were standing there staring at us. Later she told me a kindly old lady came up to her after I left and said, "Don't worry, honey, you'll be better off without him." Bonnie didn't even wait for the plane to take off. She got in the car to drive back to the apartment, and on the way back she said to herself, "They're not going to take my husband away from me again." She stopped at the bank, packed up a few things, and drove to New York.

Meanwhile, because of the weather, my plane was delayed for about four hours. When Bonnie arrived in New York she called the Holiday Inn, where I'd stayed before, but I wasn't there. Finally, the plane landed in New York and I went to the Sheraton in Hasbrouck Heights, New Jersey, and I got a telephone call. It was Bonnie. "Where have you been?" she said.

I couldn't imagine what she was talking about. Finally I asked, "Where are you?" and when she told me she was in New York, I couldn't believe it. We had four days before the Yankees went on the road. When I left to go on the road, Bonnie drove back to Syracuse, packed all our things, and carried them down the three flights of stairs. To get the TV set down, she had to rest it on her pregnant stomach for balance. The Syracuse ballplayers were on the road, so she had to make the move all by herself.

This time around with the Yankees I pitched a little more and a little better, but I never got enough work, and when I did go in, the score was usually 10–0, one way or the other. I hated to be a mop-up man. It's a dirty job, like a janitor. I dreaded going in in that situation, because whatever you do, nobody cares. They need a pigeon, and you're it. Not once did I pitch in an important situation when it counted, and for a pitcher there's a big difference between going in with the score tied and runners on base and going in losing by 10 runs. Whether you're 10 up or down, the batters are up there free-swinging. There's no pressure on them, and they swing from the heels at anything you throw up there. More often than not, they're going to hit it, too. When you're pitching in a tight situation, on the other hand, the batter has to be more selective, and your chances are much better.

Anyhow, as I said, though I didn't do spectacularly, I did much better, and I was beginning to feel that I belonged until late in the year when we played a game against the California Angels. We were losing 4–1, the bases were loaded, and Billy brought me in. I gave up a couple of nub singles, a seeing-eye hit up the middle, and they scored a few more runs to make it 8–2. No one had hit the ball hard. In the last inning we came back to score 6 to tie. Sparky ended up losing it in extra innings.

After the game I got a call in the clubhouse. George Steinbrenner wanted to see me. I didn't know why, but when I arrived at his office he was sitting there with Gabe Paul. George said, "When are you going to start pitching?"

I was astounded. "What do you mean?"

He said, "By the reports we have, you should be striking out every batter you face."

I said, "First of all, no one can do that. Second, if they'd use me right, I'd pitch better."

George said, "When we do use you, you give up run after run."

I said, "Because you have me get up in the bullpen and throw five days in a row, and then you throw me into a game and expect me to be sharp. I can't pitch that way. Nobody can."

George said, "All I know is, you better start striking out people or I'm going to ship you right back to Syracuse." Then he said, "Guidry, you will never be able to pitch in this league." And he walked out, leaving me sitting there with Gabe.

When George said, "You'll never be able to pitch in this league," I felt terrible resentment. I felt like hooking him. Everything I was trying to do he blew up right in my face. He had the nerve to chew me out like I was a puppy.

Nobody can tell me I'm not good enough to do something I want to do. In one way or another, I will prove you wrong. I will make you the heel in the end. And for him to say that in front of somebody else, that made it even more intolerable. That's something you should never do. Don't tell me I can't be a major league ballplayer, jack, because I will make you eat those words in spades. I'll do it to spite you. After he said that I thought about it and thought about it. It drove me, and it made me strive harder. I had to prove to him that I could do it.

After George walked out, I looked over at Gabe and said, "I just can't pitch the way they're making me pitch."

He said, "Don't get mad at anyone. Don't get sore. We're just trying to talk to you. Maybe you don't have what it takes. Maybe you're not mean enough."

I said, "I don't think meanness has anything to do with it. If you know how to pitch, you don't have to be mean. I'm just lacking something, but I'll find out what it is."

Gabe said, "Just go out and do the best you can, and don't worry about it."

What I was lacking was a second "out" pitch to go with my fastball. In high school, I had a curve ball, but it deserted me somewhere along the way, and the slider I had picked up was the type that broke flat away from a lefthanded hitter. For a righthander it was the easiest thing in the world to hit. I needed a better pitch.

As it turned out, the luckiest move I made was starting my Yankee career in the bullpen. Throughout my minor league career, no one had ever come over to me and said, "Ronnie, I can help you be a better pitcher." However, when I came up to the Yankees, first Dick Tidrow came over and said, "You have tremendous ability, enormous potential, all you need is another pitch and more knowledge and experience." Tidrow proceeded to teach me about pitching. Sparky Lyle then came out and began teaching me how to throw his slider. Together, the two of them made me the pitcher I am today.

Sparky taught me the mechanics. He gave me the principles behind throwing his slider, how to tug down on the ball at the end of the delivery, and day after day Sparky would watch me and check on my progress. If I was doing something wrong, he would never say, "That's not it." The only time he would say something was when I was on the right track, and then he'd urge me further. He'd say, "Now you've got the rotation down right. The ball's starting to go down. Tug a little harder on the end of your delivery and you'll have it."

Throwing in the bullpen one day, all of a sudden I found that I could throw the pitch. Now I needed to know if I could throw it in a game. As always, Sparky was there watching. Over and over he'd drum it into my head: "Pull it at the end. Don't let it fly out of your hand. Pull it down." And in his own way, he made that "pull it" sink in. He burned it into my mind.

When I had mastered the pitch, giving me the combination of a ninety-five-mile-an-hour fastball and a pitch which looked like a fastball except that it broke sharply just as it reached the plate, this was the second to last piece in the jigsaw puzzle of my success. Tidrow supplied the final piece. He stepped in and said, "Now that you have those two pitches, I'll help you with your strategy. I'll show you that pitching is more than just throwing the ball toward the plate."

More than anything else, Tidrow emphasized the importance of setting up a hitter. He told me to start out a hitter by throwing him low strikes, to get the batters thinking low. Then, he said, when you need the strikeout, you throw the fastball chest-high, and because they aren't looking for it and can't react to it quickly enough, there won't be any way they're going to hit the pitch. If the batter is lucky enough to hit it, it'll be a pop-up. Pitch 'em low and bust 'em high was Tidrow's philosophy. He also taught me how to move the ball around, not to pitch everyone the same way, and not to pitch the same way to a batter each time he comes up. He taught me that the important thing was to get the batter thinking, "What in the world is he going to throw me?" because once you have him thinking that way, you've got him. Once he's on the defensive, he's got to start guessing and commit himself early. Every once in a while, he may guess right, but not very often.

For six years I played in the Yankee farm system, and not once did I get the kind of help and advice Tidrow and Lyle gave me. All a pitching coach would say was, "Throw fifteen minutes today. Get out there and pitch." We're left alone in the minors, and this is one reason some prospects never get to the majors, because there's nobody down there to teach them anything. They just give you the ball and say, "Here, young man, go throw." So you throw. You don't pitch. They emphasize that you should throw strikes. That's a great piece of advice!

But Ron Guidry was luckier than most kids. I had two guys on my major league team who even though they knew I was fighting for their jobs said to themselves, "Here's a kid with a lot of potential. It would be a shame to let it go to waste."

I'm on a high pedestal now, and I owe so much of it to these two guys. Without them there, my skill may have drained away. We grew real close, and we'd joke that if I could give Sparky my fastball, I would, because then he and I would be the same pitcher, and every time Tidrow went out there, I wanted to give him my

en it's going to stop, but it will, and no one'll
o touch you."

though I was pitching so poorly, the Yankees
on the roster because a couple of the pitchers
rt, and they couldn't take a chance on trading a
pitcher, even if he wasn't getting anyone out.
reason the Yankees didn't trade me was Gabe.
wanted me gone, and Billy wanted me gone, but
as smarter than they were. Gabe told George,
want to trade him, you send him out with the
anding that if he ever comes back to haunt you,
ake the blame."

e based his reasoning on the fact that other clubs
nquiring about my availability. Gabe told me,
es tell me you can throw, the reports tell me you
great prospect and the other clubs tell me they
ou. How can so many people be wrong?"

season started, and a couple of weeks went by
me pitching, and then one day I went in to
guys out with no problem. I
cause
ball

pitches. I wanted to give him tha
to blow the batters away. When h
the batter, I'd watch and wish th
the ball by him, but he can't, and
it to him because he gave so much
I couldn't give them anything in
is thanks. I owe both of them so mu
wouldn't have become anything.

In 1977 I had a terrible spring t
unusual for me, because for the first
to do is strengthen my arm. I don
control or about throwing breakin
fastball after fastball. My left arm h
long time, and I know better than an
to do to get it in shape. When you
thing in the big leagues, though, the f
want to hear the excuses. All they war
you aren't pitching well.

The front office also wasn't happy

they had wanted me in the winter of 1976 to play again in Venezuela, and I refused. I told them I wouldn't go. Bonnie was almost due. They always told me, "Your family comes first," so my family came first, and they got mad at me.

My spring was a miserable one. Not only was I pitching poorly, but I pulled a muscle in my side and was out for a week. When I returned, I avoided throwing hard because I was afraid I'd tear the tendon in my arm. By not being able to throw hard, I couldn't get anybody out. Billy lost all confidence in me. One day he came up to me and said, "If there's anybody in this league you can get out, let me know, and I'll let you pitch to him." It was a real slap in the face. But while this was going on, Dick Tidrow was standing squarely behind me. Dick said, "I know it looks bad and you feel bad. You're getting hit all over, but don't you worry about it. You have too much potential to be abused like this for the rest of your career. You don't

e and got a couple of guys

using my new slider and it was working beautifully, and just as Tidrow had predicted, things were beginning to fall into place. After the game Billy was in a happy mood. He yelled over to me, "Hey, you finally got a guy out in a game."

I told Billy, "That's the guy I kept telling you about in spring training. He's the guy I can get out." We laughed, but whenever I recall Billy's earlier taunt, laughing becomes difficult.

The season progressed and we went into Kansas City, and it was one of those games where the score was 7–6 in the second inning. We had gone through five pitchers, Sparky had already pitched, so Billy brought Tidrow in. The game was close, a couple of runners were on base, and up stepped John Mayberry, who bats left-handed. Billy called down to the bullpen to find out if I was ready. I told him I was. But Billy left the right-handed Tidrow in to pitch to Mayberry—he went against the percentages—and Mayberry hit a 3-run home run to beat us.

Everyone was second-guessing Billy, saying, "I wonder why he did that?" Sparky said to me, "Why didn't he bring you in?"

I said, "I don't know. I'm not the manager. Why do you think he left me out there?"

Sparky said, "Probably because you're unproven."

I said to myself, "Damn, let me lose the game but at least go with the percentages."

The next night was an instant replay. Late in the game there was one out and two runners on base, Tidrow pitching, and up stepped George Brett, another lefty. I was warming up, and all the players were asking themselves, "Will Billy do the same thing again by letting Tidrow stay out there and go against the percentages, or will he pull the experienced guy and put the rookie in?"

I came in. I threw a fastball to Brett, who singled, but the runner was thrown out at home for the second out. With two away, I had runners on first and third, and again John Mayberry came up. It was exactly the same situation as the night before, but this time it was lefty against lefty. As I stood out on that mound, I was thinking to myself, "My job is to strike him out. That's what's expected of me. That's my reputation, that I can strike out batters with men on base." I took a deep breath. This was the first time since I joined the Yankees that a manager put me into an important situation. It was certainly the first time Billy ever trusted me. Finally, he was saying to me, "Ronnie, the game is in your hands. You're going to be either the hero or the goat."

I threw four pitches past Mayberry, three of them for strikes, and I went on to pitch two more innings of hitless ball. We scored two runs to take the lead, and when I had retired the final batter, I had my first major league victory.

The first teammate to congratulate me was Sparky. The second was Tidrow. With Sparky it was a wink and a smile, just to let me know he was thinking of me, and Tidrow did the same thing. Once we got back to the clubhouse Tidrow came over and said, "From now on it's going to be different. You'll see it."

Tidrow and I celebrated that night in the best way we knew how, eating. We wandered into a McDonald's and each ordered the customary, "four Big Macs, four French fries, and a large shake." The girl behind the counter commented, "Your family likes to eat a lot but they don't get too thirsty." We replied, "That's not for our family, that's for us." As we ate, we could see the workers looking at us in amazement. To top off a good night, we each ordered a cherry turnover for the road.

Two weeks passed before I got to pitch again. I was wondering, "I did a hell of a job. Why isn't he using me?"

We were playing Seattle on a Tuesday night, and when I arrived in the clubhouse I found a brand-new official American League ball in my locker. Gabe had traded Dock Ellis to get pitcher Mike Torrez, and when I got to the ballpark, Torrez, who was scheduled to pitch, hadn't arrived. Instead of coming to New York, he had flown home to his ailing wife in Montreal. Billy came over to me and said, "You're starting tonight."

I said, "Fine."

He said, "All I want you to do is give me 5 innings."

Sparky passed by and said to Billy, "I wouldn't be surprised if he pitched a complete-game shutout."

I went out to the mound and had a shaky first inning. I got two outs, and then a couple batters got hits, and I walked a man to load the bases. Danny Meyer, the Mariner first baseman, got up, and I had him 2 balls and 2 strikes. He's a lefty, so it was lefty against lefty, and I had the advantage, but I threw him a hanging slider. It was a bad pitch, and as soon as I threw it and he swung, I cussed at myself because I knew I had thrown a bad pitch. Fortunately, the ball flew on a line toward right field and landed foul by about the width of a coin.

I stepped behind the mound, took a deep breath, and said to myself, "Danny, you had the one chance to burn me because I threw a pitch I shouldn't have, but you blew it. You will never see that pitch again." I then threw Meyer what Sparky calls my "hellacious" slider and struck him out. I had no further problems until the ninth inning, when Sparky relieved and completed the shutout. For 8⅓ innings I had pitched shutout ball. Looking back, the strike to Meyer was probably the most important pitch of my career. Billy remarked to reporters after the game, "He had to get that one, if he didn't he might not have gotten out of the inning." But I did and finally I would get to pitch a little more now, I thought.

Two more weeks went by before I got to start another game. This time we were in Oakland, and I got to pitch because Catfish Hunter's arm was hurting him. I went into the ninth leading 2–0 and gave up two home runs. Sparky came in to relieve. We went 15 innings, and we won. I was upset, naturally, about the two home runs, but I calculated that I had pitched 16 innings and had only given up two runs.

After that game Billy put me into the starting rotation, and I never again felt like a fringe ballplayer. I beat Baltimore in my next start, again pitching a shutout into the ninth inning. For the third straight time I went 8⅓ innings. Again Sparky relieved and saved it.

When I got home that night, Bonnie was on me. "What's with the 8⅓?" she said. "When are you going to finish what you start?"

We hugged and laughed, and I told her that it wouldn't be long before Billy would let me finish.

Four times in my first six starts I worked exactly eight and a third innings. Psychologically, failure to complete a game was beginning to effect me. I began walking out to the mound to start the ninth and I was thinking about not being able to pitch more than eight and a third innings. I found myself talking subconsciously, "Ron, you know you can get three more outs."

It was not until June 16, 1977, that I was able to complete my first major league ballgame. Against Kansas City, in my seventh start of the year and sixth consecutive start of the season, I pitched my first complete game as a Yankee. In one stretch during the game, I retired seventeen in a row. I also struck out seven and recorded my first shutout. I used my imagination to overcome the jinx. As I entered the ninth inning, I kept telling myself that it was the seventh inning.

But just as quickly as I overcame the jinx, I went into a tailspin and lost three of my next four starts and it was beginning to look like I was heading back to the bullpen.

On July 23, 1977, I halted the slide against Milwaukee in a 3 to 1 victory bringing my record to 7 and 5. It was another important win for me. There had been talk of a few guys starting on three days rest and that didn't leave much for a fifth starter: me.

Suddenly, everything Sparky and Tidrow had told me came together as if by magic. One day I woke up and I *knew* what pitching was all about. I had quit throwing and had started pitching, and the slider was getting better every game and so was my control, and as I got more work I was beginning to learn for myself how to set up batters, pitching in, pitching out, experiencing for myself what Dick had taught me, pitching low, low, low, then busting one high for the strikeout. I started winning consistently, and for the first time it was fun to be playing baseball in the majors, and the thing that made it even more exciting was that the Yankees had come alive and were making a run for another pennant. When we lost a couple games, everyone was looking to me to be the stopper. They put the responsibility on my shoulders, and it was the same feeling I had had in the Colt League and in American Legion and at USL and at Syracuse. The outcome of the game was being left up to me. They were putting their faith and trust in me, and I was responding, and the more it kept on that way, the hungrier I got to produce. I couldn't wait until it was my turn to pitch again. I wanted to be out there helping the team.

I saved my best performance of the regular season for my birthday, Sunday August 28, 1977, as I pitched a two hitter versus Texas facing only twenty-eight batters in a 1–0, eight strike-out win. After the game, Bonnie and I celebrated by going back home to New Jersey and throwing two steaks on the grill and drinking champagne, courtesy of George Steinbrenner.

It was only a few days later that I received the vote of confidence from Billy Martin that I needed. In early September, we beat the Indians, 4–3, in ten innings. It was the kind of game that would have been easy for Billy to remove me early. He stayed with me through ten tough innings. He stayed with me through a two-run first and a one-run fourth. He stayed with me even though the Indians tagged me for eight hits and three walks in the first six innings.

The timing of Billy's expression of confidence was important. One week later, we faced the Boston Red Sox in the opener of a three-game series that would make the season, that would win the pennant for us.

I spent the afternoon of the game romping around the house with my daughter Jamie. I also found time to think about the times I had faced Boston in the past. I reminded myself that I was not the same pitcher the Red Sox had pounded during spring training the year before. Ten pitches into the game, the Red Sox had a pretty good idea of the type pitcher I had become. They were all strikes and they took care of the top third of the line-up. After 130 more pitches, I was able to complete a five-hit, 4–2 victory before the second largest crowd ever to fill the Yankee Stadium, 55,269.

I enjoyed the various comments my performance received from the Boston players. George Scott, Boston's first baseman at the time and later to be a teammate on the 1979 Yankees, said, "Early in the game he showed me what he's made of, I had him 3–1 in the fourth inning and I expected a fastball, but I got a slider for a strike. Then he took something off the fastball and got me to pop to right field. He works in and out. He's more than a thrower." Thanks, George. Jim Rice was a little more critical. He disagreed vehemently with Scott. "He's got speed and nothing else. He showed me nothing. We lost because of the ballpark. We're supposed to be playing in a ballpark, not the Grand Canyon." I've always wondered if Rice's opinion of my pitching was still the same after his two for thirteen performance against me in 1978.

I had little time to savor the Boston victory for shortly thereafter the Yankees were in the American League playoffs against the Kansas City Royals.

We lost the first game, and again in the second game I had the opportunity to be the stopper. In my only appearance during that series, I held the Royals to three hits while striking out seven as the Yankees won 6–2.

I felt overpowering. Whitey Herzog, the Kansas City manager sensed it also. "I knew the way the kid was pitching, it was going to be tough to score," he said. One of the hits was an infield grounder and another was a cracked bat hit. The third was clean. In one inning, they scored a run without getting a hit.

It was now time for the World Series. Time to discover what it was like pitching in front of millions of viewers all over the world. In the brief hours before the most important pitching assignment of my life, I took a walk with Bonnie, did some shopping and talked about the things any young couple would talk about. The only discussion we had about the game was Bonnie telling me "Don't scratch yourself because millions of people will be watching you." I told Bonnie before the game, "I won't be upset if I lose as long as I don't embarrass myself." I wouldn't have been too terribly disappointed if I had lost 1–0, figuring that's the way it goes. I did not want to lose 12–0 however.

Fortunately, I pitched a good game, won 4–2, allowing four hits. It was a big thrill for me to pitch that game. Everybody's first World Series game is the most important in their baseball career. Against the Dodgers, I held the big hitters in check. I threw hard, had a great slider. I made one mistake the whole game, and Davey Lopes hit it out. The only other legitimate hit was Rick Rhoden's double. One hit was a grounder down third that Nettles said was foul by six inches but the umpire said was fair, but what can you do? The other was a grounder that bounced off Graig's glove. The key play of the game was a great catch by Piniella up against the wall. It settled me down, and after that it was a piece of cake.

I found it hard to believe, but in one year I had experienced the thrill of accomplishing goals I had set when I was young, of winning in the majors, of pitching in a World Series before 56,000 people in the stands and millions more watching on television. I finished the year with a 16–7 record, had a 2.82 earned-run average, and pitched 5 shutouts. Not bad for a guy who was told by his owner that he'd never make it as a major-leaguer and who was told by his manager, "If there's a batter you can get out, tell me who it is, and I'll let you pitch to him." And as I look back on this, I can't help but think that if Bonnie hadn't agreed to go back to Syracuse one more time, none of this would have happened.

6

The Girl of My Dreams

After I won the Cy Young award the next year, Jack Lang, secretary of the New York Chapter of the Baseball Writers Association, called to invite me to the writers' annual dinner in New York. I asked him, "I can bring Bonnie, can't I?"

Traditionally the dinner has been a stag affair, and so Lang hemmed and hawed and said, "You know, Ronnie, that women are not invited."

I said, "Mr. Lang, if Bonnie can't come, then I'm not coming either."

He hemmed and hawed a little more, and then he gave in. "I guess we can find a spot for her," he said.

At the dinner, I was invited to say a few words and I recounted our conversation to the audience. I wanted everyone there to understand just how important Bonnie had been to my success, and I wanted it known that I would not stand for anyone treating Bonnie with less respect than they accorded me. I said: "For those of you who don't know her and who don't have the good fortune to be married to her, Bonnie is the one who should be standing up here receiving this award, because without her I wouldn't be here." And I asked her to stand up and take a bow. I wanted everyone to know exactly how I felt about the males-only policy, and I sat down. I'm not sure how the writers felt about what I had to say, but that's how I felt, and if they didn't like it, it's too bad. Too many times baseball excludes the wives. But no one is going to exclude Bonnie.

I met Bonnie when I was a freshman at USL. It was late August, and I was pitching in an American Legion game, and Bonnie's boyfriend at the time was playing on the other team. Throughout the game I kept hearing this young girl shouting, "Take the skinny guy out. He's no good. Hey, pitch, you look like a coat hanger." Things like that. I'm out there pitching, minding my own business, and I didn't know who the hell she was, never noticed her before, and here she's calling me skinny and ugly and screaming and hollering and carrying on.

The game ended—I had pitched a 1-hit shutout—and I went over to my friend Boo Menard and asked him, "Who was the girl in the stands that kept yelling after me? What the hell have I done to her?"

Boo said she was a cheerleader at the high school.

As we left the field, I was watching this loud-mouthed girl walking away, and I said to Boo, "She's got a big mouth, but she's got a nice figure. They didn't make girls like that when I was going to high school." Boo told me her name, but it went in one ear and out the other.

The next week was the American Legion banquet. The season was over, and at the end of the year we all got together for an awards ceremony. I already had a date for the banquet, but a few days before the dinner my date called me up to say that her dad had died and she wouldn't be able to go. I called Boo and told him what had happened, and we were talking, and he said, "You know who you ought to go out with?"

"Who?"

"Bonnie Rutledge."

I said, "Who is that?"

He said, "You remember that girl you saw the other day at the ballgame, the one you said had a nice-looking figure?" I hadn't remembered. He continued, "Wait, I'll show you her picture in the yearbook." He started going through the book to find her picture.

Well, in Bonnie's four years of high school, that picture is the ugliest one. Every other picture showed her to be beautiful, with long straight hair. But in this one, she looked terrible. I said, "Boo, what are you trying to do?"

He said, "She doesn't really look like that. This picture should be banned. It doesn't do her justice." Then Boo said something that made me think twice, because Boo was quite a lady's man. He said, "I'll tell you what I'll do. You take my date, and I'll take Bonnie."

If he was willing to give her up for Bonnie, I figured that Bonnie must be A-O.K. I said, "Well, I don't know, Boo. I guess I'll take Bonnie."

Boo said, "Call her on the phone and talk to her, and then I'll talk to her for a while." At that time I had a very heavy Cajun accent, and when she picked up the phone, I said, "This is Ronnie Guidry," and that was all she understood for the next five minutes. Bonnie kept saying, "What? What?" She couldn't understand a word I was saying. I still insist she didn't understand because she was so shook up that I had called, but finally Boo got on the phone and asked her if she would go out with me, and she agreed. When we got off the phone, I said to Boo, "You understood what I was saying, didn't you?" He had. "Maybe there's something wrong with her," I thought. "Maybe she doesn't hear right."

The banquet was Saturday night, and I called Bonnie that afternoon to ask her if she wanted to go riding with me to get a Dr Pepper. I said, "Boo and I'll come and get you so we can get acquainted before we got out on our date."

Bonnie said, "Okay, but I'm warning you, I have my hair up in curlers."

I said, "No matter," and so Boo and I went over to her house and when she came to the door her hair was rolled up in beer cans! I looked at her, and I looked at Boo like: "Wait till we get home, sucker."

I was driving a convertible, with bucket seats, and I had the top down, and we drove over to the local hamburger joint with Bonnie sitting between Boo and me and all the college kids were there, and her hair was up in beer cans. I was scrunched down in my seat so no one could see me with her.

When we got home, I said to Boo, "No way I should have let you talk me into going out with her. She looks like she has a pretty face but, man, it's hard to be sure." She looked like she was ready to go into battle.

That night I went back to Bonnie's house to pick her up for the banquet, and I went through the customary introductions with her mom and dad. She was only a sophomore, and I was in college, and since I was taking her out for the first time, they were checking me out,

108

trying to see whether I was one of those college guys who was going to take her out to smoke dope and take advantage of her. I was sitting there trying to be casual, but it was difficult, because whenever I looked I could see her mother staring at me. Finally her mom said, "Bonnie, Ronnie's here," and I'm thinking to myself, "I don't want to go," because all I could see were those Budweiser cans in her hair, but I could not describe how beautiful she looked when she came out. She had beautiful hair that hung down her back, and her dress came down to about her knees. I was stunned. I couldn't say a word. I didn't want to say, "Jesus Christ, you look beautiful," because I didn't know if she would have wanted to hear that from a guy she barely knew. I decided to try and act calm and cool, which I did, even though I was ready to flip out.

We drove to the banquet, and as we were sitting there listening to the speeches, I put my hand on her knee, and her knee jerked up so hard she nearly spilled my soda. Boo and I went over to get something to drink, and he said, "What the heck happened at the table. You look like you got scared."

"Damn, I just touched her on the leg and I thought she was going to knock the table over." Later that evening she told me, "When you put your hand on my leg, you gave me such a thrill." I cracked up. I laughed for two weeks.

The week after the banquet I asked Bonnie to go steady, and she agreed. She wore my ring. We ended up going steady for a week and a half. Bonnie's mom didn't like the idea of our going steady. I was in college and she was just a sixteen-year-old sophomore, and I was coming over to her house every afternoon, and Bonnie's mom was afraid her daughter was going to run off and get married before she finished high school. So after about ten days she gave me the ring back and started going out with other guys as well as with me.

In her junior year she started dating a football player. I found this out from Boo. He came up to me and said, "Guess who Bonnie's going out with?"

I said, "Who?" in a way that made me sound like I was pretending not to care.

"The flashy halfback on the football team all the girls are drooling over."

I said, "Is Bonnie going steady with him?"

Boo said, "I don't know, but I think it's serious."

I said, "No problem. One less person to call." That's what I said, but I can assure you, my heart was broken. My Cajun pride, though, was not going to let anyone know.

A week later, Boo called. "Guess what happened in school today?" he said. Boo was a year older than Bonnie. He was a senior, and they were in the same journalism class.

"What happened, Boo?" I asked.

"A guy asked Bonnie out, and her football player said to him, 'You can't ask her, because we're going steady,' and Bonnie hit the roof. She told him, 'Don't you tell people we're going steady when we're not. I can go out with anybody I want, and I don't want to go out with you anymore."

As unhappy as I was the week before, that's how happy I was when he told me that. That night I called her and we went out and had a wonderful time, and the next day Boo said, "Did you have a date with Bonnie last night?"

"Yeah, why?"

"Damn, let me warn you. That football player is looking all over town for you. He wants to fight you."

"What the hell for?"

"Because you went out with Bonnie."

"You told me Bonnie didn't want to go out with him anymore?"

"But he doesn't see it that way."

"What should I do?"

"I hate to see you go over there, because we don't want to have to send for the ambulance to pick up the pieces."

"He's that tough?"

"No, dummy, I was talking about calling the ambulance for him."

"I don't want to fight the guy."

"We don't want you to either, cause we need the guy on the football team. He's good."

"Boo, I'm not going to worry about it."

A couple days later I was invited to a party. I went with another girl, and Bonnie was with her football player, and naturally Bonnie and I ran into each other, so we started talking. And her date got mad. He was over getting a drink, and I walked over to him and tapped him on the shoulder. He was about six feet and two hundred pounds, but Boo had told me that if I acted tough, he would back down. I said real tough, "Somebody told me you were looking for me."

"Oh no. I'm not looking for you."

"If you need me for anything, I'm not hard to find. Just ask for Ronald."

"Don't worry, I won't need you for anything." That was it. I never had any more trouble.

Except that Bonnie and I didn't go out anymore. I went to Liberal the summer of my sophomore year to play semi-pro ball, and while I was there I began going with another girl. I didn't keep in touch with Bonnie at all, though her friend Kathy would always write to me about her. I never asked Kathy about Bonnie. I was still interested in how she was doing, because I still liked her a great deal, but when you like somebody as much as I did, you don't want to go around asking about her all the time. But Kathy kept me informed. Meanwhile, I ran into a girl I spent a lot of time with, whom I really liked, and at the end of August, when semi-pro ball was over, I asked her if she wanted to come to Louisiana to visit. I liked this girl very much, but I didn't know if it was love. It turned out that she was the complete opposite of me. She told me she wasn't sure she wanted to leave Kansas City because her roots were there. I told her I'd call her in a couple of weeks to find out if she wanted to come to Louisiana

111

to see me. When I called, she said she couldn't come. I said to myself, "Maybe this isn't going to work out." It didn't.

When I got home, I dated Bonnie two or three times. One night in December I brought her home, and it was one of those times when everything was going smoothly, but apparently I sneezed when I shouldn't have, or she said good-bye when she should have said hello, and when I dropped her home at the doorstep, we had a difference, and that was it. I didn't talk to her again until the end of May.

I was drafted by the Yankees in June, and I'm packing to go to Johnson City, and my mom comes over and says to me, "What are you going to do about Bonnie?" I said, "Who?" We hadn't spoken in five months. And about this time Bobby Badeaux, who had been in Vietnam, came home on a thirty day leave. I was so glad to see him. The first day back home he said, "Ronnie, tomorrow let's go out to the shopping mall and just look at the girls." So the next day we drove out to the mall and had eyestrain, that's how hard we were looking at the girls. We were walking back to the car, and all of a sudden Bobby whispered to me, "Get me a chair. I've got to sit down. Look at the figure on that girl!" I looked, and all I could see was this gorgeous pair of legs walking along. We started to follow her. She went over to one of the store windows, and I was watching her from behind. I never thought a girl could look so good. We were walking slowly to get a better look, and she straightened up and turned around, and she saw Bobby and me, and my brain started to burn up. It fizzled. It was Bonnie. As I stood there dumbfounded, Bonnie ran up to Bobby, who had been hurt in Vietnam, and she was so happy to see him that she ignored me completely. We went to a coffee shop and drank Coke and talked for an hour, and all Bobby and Bonnie talked about was Bobby's girlfriend Kathy. For an hour, the only thing I had said was, "Hi, what's happening?" Finally, I said to Bobby, "We got to go," and Bobby said, "Wait one minute. I'll be right back." So Bonnie and I were sitting there, and we didn't say a word. I was just not going to say something to her. We had been there for an hour, and she hadn't said anything to me.

We got up to wait for Bobby, and she grabbed me by the arm and said, "Why don't you call me sometime?"

Bonnie knew I was going to Johnson City in a week, and I guess she figured she'd better make a move quick. So that night I called her. We went out almost every night before I left. We were on good terms when I left, and we'd write, and sometimes I'd send her flowers. When the season was over, I went right into the National Guard, so from June until mid-December we didn't see each other at all. But when I got home in mid-December, I asked Bonnie if she wanted to get engaged, and she said yes. Then I left for the rest of basic training, and after that it was off to spring training and another summer of baseball. We were engaged nine months, and we might have seen each other maybe ten times. I returned from my year at Fort Lauderdale in August and we got married in September.

The night before the wedding, we had a rehearsal, and then Bobby and a couple of other friends and I drove to New Orleans. The ceremony was scheduled for one in the afternoon, and we had stayed out all night. We came roaring back home and pulled into my house at about twelve-thirty. The clothes were flying every which way. The four of us dressed at my house, and it was ten miles from my house to the church, and when we arrived we could hear the organist playing.

At the reception it's a Cajun custom to pin money on the bride's veil before you dance with her. Bonnie didn't know this. One of the guests began pinning money on Bonnie, and she looked at him strangely as if to say, "What are you doing?" He explained. Later Bonnie told me, "I didn't know what he was paying me for. I hadn't done anything."

I had hidden my car at the home of one of my relatives because I was afraid of what my friends were going to do with it, and in the middle of the reception, Grandpa Gus drove Bonnie and me out into the country, where we had hidden the car. There was no Interstate 10 at that time, and I drove my GTO for an hour and a half at seventy miles an hour to reach New Orleans. Normally it takes two and a half hours. We got to the hotel—it was the Court of the Two Sisters in the old part of New Orleans—we took the elevator to our room, and I couldn't get the damn door open. You had to push a little button at the same time you turned the key. I didn't know how to work it, so I had to go back downstairs to get some help to get into the room. I just couldn't open that door. I don't go to a hotel room every night. What the hell, you don't get married every day.

7

Don't Tell Me I Can't Pitch

During spring training in 1977, I pitched terribly, as I usually do in spring training, so I was belittled, and there was talk of my being traded, but in spring training 1978, I came to camp with the flu, reported a week late, and didn't pitch until a week later, and when I did pitch I was terrible, but this time nobody cared. Why? Because I was a nobody in '77, but in '78 I was coming back a 16-game winner. Does that make any sense at all? If management would treat every untested rookie as though he had won 16 games the year before, a lot more of them would make the majors sooner. Show some confidence in the young guys. That's all many of them need to make it.

When I began the 1978 season I didn't have to prove anything. I didn't have to prove I could pitch out of jams. I didn't have to prove I could go nine innings. I was able to go out to the mound and not worry, and Billy showed confidence in me by letting me pitch opening day. In other words, I felt he was telling me he thought I was his best pitcher. I wanted to justify his confidence.

Though I was 16–7 in 1977, if you looked closely, you'd see that I was 6–5 before the All-Star break, and 10–2 afterward. As the season went on I was becoming a much better pitcher, and I figured that all I had to do to start the 1978 season was to pick up where I left off. And I did. The team was playing good ball, and if I allowed two runs we'd score three, and my confidence began to build and build, and every time I went out there I figured I was going to win. I'd say to myself, "I ain't losing this game no matter what happens. I ain't losing." And I wouldn't. I ran my record to 13–0 with a 1.75 earned-run average before I lost a game in early July.

We were in Milwaukee, and my arm was really tired. It was the last game I was scheduled to pitch before the All-Star break, and I knew I needed a rest, but after pondering whether to go to Billy and ask him to pass me by this once, I figured that I had gone this far without losing and that I could somehow bluff my way through and get by. Also, we had fallen way behind Boston, and I figured we'd have our best shot at winning the game if I pitched, so I went ahead. It was a mistake. Mike Caldwell was pitching for the Brewers, and because he pitched a shutout, there was no way we were going to win the game, but when I went out there I had nothing on the ball, so we lost 6–0.

I was not invincible, even though for most of the season I had felt that way.

Everything had gone right. My fastball and slider both exploded, and I had good control over both pitches, and when I'd make a bad pitch, the batter would hit a long foul or my fielders would make great plays, and it was like being in heaven. I even won a game after swallowing my chewing tobacco.

We were playing Baltimore, and I had a big wad in my mouth. Rich Dauer hit a high-hopping ball out over the mound, and I jumped for it, and when I hit the ground, it was a quick, involuntary reflex. I gulped down the chewing tobacco. I had an 8–0 lead at the time, and after pitching another inning, I felt nauseous, so I asked Billy to take me out. That was the worst problem I had all year.

The highlight of the season was probably the game against California in which I struck out 18 batters. I went into the game with a 10–0 record. We were playing at Yankee Stadium, and it was a muggy night, but it was cooling fast. Usually when I'd leave the bullpen to begin the game, Sparky would ask me, "How does it feel?" and on this night I said, "Jesus, man, tonight I've got nothing." And I went out there, and sure enough, the first batter doubled, I struck out the next batter, I made a lucky stop on a hard-hit ball up the middle and threw the batter out for the second out, and I struck out the next guy. In the second inning I struck out one more, and I got two in the third, so I had six strikeouts. It was that sixth strikeout that was the catalyst in the

117

chain of events that made me realize this night would be different from any other night in my major league career to date.

I had gotten two quick strikes on Rudi, then I threw him smoke, my 96 miles per hour "seed" and Joe Rudi never had a chance. That was strikeout number six, and that was the one. From that moment on, strikeouts were the thing. The capacity crowd became alive, standing and applauding, cheering in thrilled anticipation, whenever I got two strikes on the batter. It pumped me up and it tended to make the batter a little nervous; the batter couldn't concentrate on hitting with all that noise. I wanted to give the people what they paid for. When I got two strikes on the batter, I began to challenge him with fast balls that were tailing, sailing, and sinking, and sliders that dropped and darted away from the Angel hitters. I struck out the side on the fourth, fifth, and sixth giving me a total of fourteen for the game. In the seventh, I struck out Brian Downing for the third out, number fifteen, the one that tied Bob Shawkey's Yankee record and I broke it when I struck out the lead-off batter in the eighth. The fact that I broke the Yankee record is amazing, considering the outstanding pitchers that this club has had throughout the many years: Whitey Ford, Eddie Lopat, "Lefty" Gomez, Red Ruffing, Allie Reynolds.

Entering the ninth inning, I was out to match the Major League Record held by Steve Carlton, Tom Seaver and Nolan Ryan of 19 strikeouts. I needed three. The first two batters went down on strikes, Rudi for the fourth time. I had one left. One shot at the record and when Don Bailor sent a sinking liner to center, I too sighed with relief even though the ball dropped for a hit. This gave me one more chance. But Ron Jackson hit my first pitch to third baseman Craig Nettles, and the record was safe—this time. "That's alright," said Munson, "you can't do everything in one night, you have to save something for next time." And there would be a next time, another chance. I felt proud to hear other ballplayers comment on my performance. "He'll strike out 19 some night," Billy Martin said confidently. "He'll strike out more than 19. I'm sure of it. It's just a matter of time."

"They were choking up on the bat, swinging defensively," boasted Dick Tidrow, my roommate on the road, "their big power hitters were choking up just trying to meet the ball, and they couldn't do it."

In the other dugout, Nolan Ryan, who had one-third of the record I was chasing, stated: "The entire bench was laughing because we felt we were overmatched." "You know what he said in the bullpen before the game?" Sparky Lyle volunteered. "He said he didn't think he had it tonight. You guys are in for a real treat when he does have it."

But, that's what pitching is all about, to stand out there and throw and challenge guys and have them swing and miss. It's the ultimate feeling for a pitcher. I made good pitches, and they couldn't hit them. I made bad pitches, and they couldn't hit them either. I threw sliders in the dirt, and they swung and missed. I threw fast balls in the sky and they swung and made out. Everything I threw, they swung at. And missed. They were so intent on *not* striking out that they did. Guys were choking up on the bat, trying to make contact, and they were abandoning their natural swing, and they were messing themselves up.

And from that night on, the fans were something else too. Every time I would have two strikes on a batter, they would begin stomping and shouting and cheering and carrying on, and it made my adrenaline flow, and it got so that if I didn't strike out the batter, they would boo; though I didn't really know whether they were booing me or booing the batter.

That night I also was tagged with the nickname Louisiana Lightning. A young fan had hung a banner from the railing of Yankee Stadium with a map of Louisiana engraved on it and a lightning bolt flashing across the state with the words "Louisiana Lightning" across the top. Phil Rizzuto, the Yankee announcer, noticed the sign and in his natural enthusiasm adopted the slogan as my tag. It stuck ever since.

The California game did take its physical toll. Because injuries had severely hampered our pitching staff in the early part of the season, I was the only Yankee pitcher who hadn't missed a single start. This was the most innings I had ever pitched in pro ball, and if my arm was tired before the California game, after it the arm was crying for a rest.

Ordinarily the first thing I do immediately after pitching is to put my arm in ice for twenty minutes. Despite that, by the next day my arm is so sore I can barely lift a coffee cup. For two days after every start I become a righthander. By the third day the soreness begins to go, and I loosen up by pitching batting practice. I relax on day four, and by day five I'm raring to go again.

After the California game, I could have used a whole week of rest, but I couldn't get it because we were battling back to catch Boston, and I had to pitch as often as possible. For the next few outings, I struggled. Though I beat the Tigers the next game out to go 12 and 0, I failed to strike out at least ten batters as I had been doing. Then against Boston, I only went six innings, giving up four runs. Fortunately, Graig Nettles homered to give us an extra-inning win.

Atley Donald, a fellow Louisianian and the man who signed me, had set the Yankee record for 12 consecutive wins, and on July 2, I battled the Tigers' Dave Rosema in an attempt to set a new record at 13.

Ron LeFlore hit a long home run in the first inning, and after that Rosema and I battled until it was 1–0 Detroit in the bottom of the ninth.

Sitting in the dugout, I was preparing myself mentally for the reality of my first defeat of the year. Reggie Jackson, who was the second batter, came over to me. "Here's where I pay you back," he said referring to an earlier game where he misjudged a fly and spoiled my shutout. After that game he came over and promised he'd make it up to me.

Reggie stepped in against Rosema, and he poled a long home run into the right field stands. As he rambled around the bases in his home run trot, I sat in that dugout with tears streaming down my cheeks. When he came into the dugout, amid the backslapping and words of congratulations, he looked at me and gave me a wink, and he said, "We're even." I smiled back. We scored two more runs to win, and I had my record.

I've always liked Reggie. We didn't become close immediately because we both proceed cautiously in developing new friendships. As the years passed, however, we became close. He respects my pitching, and I respect his hitting. Any man who tells you he's going to do something and then goes out and does it, you have to like and respect that. Still, there are times when I have cardiac arrest when he's out in right field.

One time I was pitching to a left-handed batter who lined the ball into right field. Reggie evidently misjudged the ball or lost it in the lights, but he got a slow jump on the ball. He had to rush in quickly, and at the last second he dove and made a great catch. The fans went wild. The guys on the team, however, knew that Reggie had made an easy play look difficult. On the bus back to the hotel after the game Reggie was sitting with—and this may surprise you—Thurman, and Thurman was riding Reggie unmercifully about his defense. Reggie, in his own defense, reminded Thurman about his diving catch. Thurman laughed. I was sitting in the front of the bus, happy not to be involved in their conversation but enjoying it nevertheless. But Reggie decided to bring me in as an impartial third party. He'd have been better off with ten Billy Martins on the jury. He asked me what I thought of the catch.

Deadpanned, I said, "Honestly, Reggie, I didn't see the play. I had my glove over my face the entire time."

Reggie quickly changed the subject.

It was in the next game that Mike Caldwell shut us out 6–0. The setback, though, was short-lived. I only lost three games that year, all to pitchers named Mike:

Caldwell, Willis of Toronto, and Flannigan of Baltimore.

That year, of course, was also a year of great turmoil on the Yankees. George had acquired Reggie Jackson during the winter of 1976, and from the day he joined us in 1977 there was trouble. First it was between Reggie and Thurman Munson. Thurman was a winner, a stiff competitor who liked to be out front. He liked his name to be on the top of the marquee. But when Reggie came to the club, it became clear that Reggie wanted to be recognized as the best. He'd walk into the room with his shoulders held way back to say that, hey, Reggie Jackson is here. He wants to be recognized for who he is, and I can understand that. But when he came here, he made some comments that suggested Thurman wasn't the leader Thurman felt he was, and there was bad feeling from the start. Then Billy Martin and Reggie got to feuding. Billy just didn't think Reggie was as good a player as Reggie thought he was, and then when Billy asked Reggie to do certain things, Reggie wouldn't do them. It was a battle of egos, and the more it went on the worse it got, until Billy had enough and finally quit in the middle of the season.

In my opinion the biggest problem the two of them had was that they were always talking to the newspaper reporters. When you're a ballplayer, people are watching you, and it's their job to talk to you and get information to print in the papers. They ask you questions, but there are different ways to answer a question. You don't have to volunteer information. When a reporter asks a question, I give enough information to answer that question and no more. And if I don't like the question, I don't answer. Neither of them know how to keep out of trouble in the papers.

With a team of twenty-five players, there are bound to be disagreements. There will be shouting matches, because everyone can't be happy all the time. Throughout that controversy I had a policy that stood me in good stead. I would keep my mouth shut. My job was to go out on that mound every fifth day, and that's what

I did. That's what I'm paid to do. The rest of it I left to the other guys.

When Billy left and Bob Lemon took over it helped us at that time, because we needed some rest and relaxation from what had been going on, we needed some calm because the tension was high, and we got it. For myself, it didn't matter to me who the manager was. All I wanted was for the manager to give me the ball and send me out to the mound. I pitched just as well for Lemon as I had for Martin, and that's all that mattered to me. I wanted to make sure nothing would upset my routine, my rhythm. I said to myself, "If they want to change managers twenty times, let them. I won't worry about it."

During the first week in September I beat the Tigers 9–1 to win my twentieth game against two losses, and by this time we had closed the gap with Boston from 14 to 5 games. My next two starts were against the Red Sox, and on September 9, I pitched a two-hit shutout up at Fenway Park, then on September 15, I pitched another two-hit shutout, as the Yankees won four in a row and then two out of three to take over first place. When we tied Boston for first that weekend, I knew then that we would win the pennant, and we did. We had come from too far back to lose.

The key element in our victory, in my opinion, was the return to form of Catfish Hunter. When Cat was right, he was one of the best pitchers of all time. He was phenomenal. However, the last couple of years Cat had been plagued by arm trouble and wasn't the same pitcher. I'd sit in the dugout while he was pitching, and I'd be afraid to watch, he'd get roughed up so badly. Once in Boston he gave up four home runs in the first inning. And yet to me Cat represented class. A guy would hit a home run, and he'd stand on that mound, and he would never change his expression. And he was still certain he'd get the next guy out.

The thing that impressed me more than anything was that I could go out there and blow guys away, and I'd never break a bat. The hardest thing for me is to break a guy's bat. But Cat would go out there and throw his stuff, and he'd jam the batters and at least twice a game he'd break their bats. He'd throw those pitches at sixty miles an hour and make the batters look as bad as Goose Gossage or I would. I'd always kid Cat. I'd say, "You shouldn't pitch, because you embarrass me that you can get the guys out and make 'em look bad and I can't. How can you get guys out with that junk you throw?" He'd laugh, but he did get them out, and at the end of the 1978 season he won about nine in a row, and without him, we'd never have had a chance at the pennant.

I won my twenty-fourth game 3–1 against the Blue Jays pitching with only three days rest. Lem set up the rotation that way, figuring that if we finished in a tie with the Red Sox I'd be able to start the playoff game. We beat Cleveland two out of three, but the Red Sox won their last three games, and there was a tie, and I was ready.

We played THE GAME at Fenway Park, and the only thing that worried me was that because I was pitching with only three days rest I wouldn't be strong enough, and you had to be strong with that short porch in left field in Fenway. I didn't have my best stuff, but I was strong enough. They scored the first run in the second inning. I threw Yastrzemski a pitch that was way inside and high, and he tomahawked it and hit it just inside the right-field foul pole. We saw pictures of his swing later, and I still can't believe he was able to hit that pitch. In the sixth Burleson doubled, he was sacrificed to third, and Rice singled up the middle. That made the score 2–0. Even then I really wasn't worried. An out and an intentional walk put men on first and second, two outs, and Fred Lynn at bat. When Lynn yanked one of my sliders into the rightfield corner I thought: "Two runs!" But rightfielder Lou Piniella was playing far over to his left, and he was able to make the catch.

Many people have commented that Piniella was so far out of position for Lynn that he had to have ESP. Lynn was the one most convinced of this. "It was a ridiculous place for him to be . . . about 20 yards from where he normally plays me." I would have agreed, but two innings before, Munson, Piniella and I talked and we agreed that my slider was losing speed and getting easier to pull. So we agreed that Lou would shade toward the line.

We had just beaten them four in a row in Fenway, and they knew we could score a bunch of runs any inning, it was just a matter of time before they cracked. They did, too. In the seventh we got singles by Chris Chambliss and Roy White, and Bucky Dent, who had hit only four home runs all season, went up and hit a home run into the left-field screen for three runs. Micky Rivers singled, stole second, and scored on Thurman's double, and we had them 4–2.

When I'm pitching, I'm concentrating so much on what I have to do that I'm not really excited about what's going on. When Dent hit it out, all I knew was that now we had the lead and that I had to hold them.

In the bottom of the inning, I struck out Butch Hobson. With George Scott up, the coaches thought I was losing my stuff, so they had the infield playing farther to the left than usual, and Scott hit a grounder that just went past where Brian Doyle would have been had he been in his usual spot. Lem came out to the mound and took me out even though I really didn't want to go. I told him, "Lem, I'm still strong," but he raised his right arm and signaled for Goose Gossage to come in, and Goose got out of the inning.

Reggie hit what many of us thought was an insurance home run in the top of the eighth to make the score 5–2, but it turned out to be the difference. In the bottom of the inning the Red Sox scored twice to make it 5–4.

The ninth inning was a heart-stopper. I was in the clubhouse soaking my arm in ice and watching it on television. Goose got the first batter, but Burleson walked. Jerry Remy was the next batter, and if Bucky's home run was the offensive play of the game, Lou Piniella's play on Remy was the defensive. Remy hit an

0–2 pitch toward right field in Lou's direction. Everyone watching could see the ball, but Lou had no idea where it was as it came his way. The sun was blinding him.

But if Piniella is anything, he's lucky. We all kid him about his being such a lucky guess-hitter. As the ball started to descend, Burleson held his ground at first, believing that Lou would catch it, and Lou gave no indication that he wouldn't as he stood waiting for it. When the ball bounced eight feet in front of him, it was too late for Burleson to go to third. If he had, he would have scored the tying run on Rice's long fly ball. As it was, Burleson could only tag on Rice's fly and go to third, and that's where he died.

With two outs and Burleson on third, Yaz was the batter. In the locker room everything stopped. No one talked. It was tough enough to breathe. When Yaz popped out to Nettles at third, everyone exhaled. We were the champions.

Lost in the excitement was the fact that it was my twenty-fifth win of the season against only three losses. When I beat Kansas City 2–1 in the playoffs and beat the Dodgers 5–1 in the series, my season statistics were beyond even my own comprehension. In the 35 times I started, the Yankees won 30 times. Opposing batters hit .193 against me. I had nine shutouts, the most in the American League in one season since Babe Ruth did it in 1916. Fifteen of my wins followed Yankee losses. I struck out 10 batters in a game eight times. I won 12 of my last 14 games with an earned-run average of 1.28. I struck out 248 batters, beating Jack Chesbro's record that he set in 1904. Finally, my .893 winning percentage was the highest in baseball history for a 20-game winner, and my 1.74 earned-run average for the season was second in American League history for a lefthander (Dutch Leonard had a 1.01 ERA in 1914).

It was an awesome year, and I knew there were going to be aspects of my life that would change as a result of this, aspects I would not be comfortable with. All of a sudden people I didn't know knew me, and when Bonnie and I would go out for dinner, people would be asking for autographs in the middle of our dinner, and at first I would oblige, but then it began to happen all the time, and after a while I'd ask, "Would you mind waiting until after I eat?" Most of the people would wait, but some would get mad. Pretty soon we had to go only to restaurants where we knew the owner and get a table in the corner where no one would notice us. Then when we got home to Lafayette, we figured we could go on just like before, but we couldn't. We'd go to the movies, and people would climb over the seats in the middle of the picture to ask for an autograph. Pretty soon we stopped going out so much, and we just stayed home.

The worst thing is that now that I am someone who is known, my own relatives sometimes feel they can't just pop over the way they used to. Now they call before they come, or they feel they have to make an appointment. Some of them treat us like they used to, but some of them don't, and it really bothers me.

I don't want people staring at me or making a fuss over me, but since that 25–3 season I have to put up with it. What also bothers me is that a lot of people who come up to me now and try to know me will disappear just as soon as I stop playing baseball.

My 1978 superseason also had an effect on me the next year. During the off-season, I thought I handled the pressure pretty well. Reporters would always be asking me, "What are you going to do for an encore?" and my stock reply would be, "There's no way I could have another year like I had last year. A year like that comes along once in a lifetime." The other thing I'd tell them was, "If I only win one game next year, but it's the game that gets us into the World Series, I'll have had a good year."

The pressure was there once the season started. The year before I had gone 13 wins before I lost a game, and this year in the opening day of the season I pitched a perfect game for six innings, but then I lost the game, and I started to press. I lost my mental control over the

127

game. I wasn't pitching intelligently. Instead, I was reaching back, trying to throw a little harder than was natural, and my control was off, and I was getting hit more often. I lost a couple more games early, and what made it worse was that the team as a whole was playing poorly. Making things tougher, Goose Gossage pitched a game in relief, got hit and lost, and after the game a reporter was asking Cliff Johnson whether he had hit Gossage when they were both in the National League, and Gossage replied before Cliff could answer, "He swung at what he heard," and then Cliff said something and threw a piece of masking tape at him, and Gossage threw it back, and for a while that was that. The two of them then went into the bathroom, and Cliff gave Goose a playful shove, and Goose, who was angry, slapped at Cliff, and they got into a fight and Goose hurt his hand badly. With Sparky Lyle traded to Texas and Dick Tidrow ineffective, our bullpen was a disaster area after that. We must have lost ten games we might have won had Goose not gotten hurt.

In late April we were coming off a disastrous road trip to the Coast, and I went to pitching coach Tom Morgan and suggested that he put me in the bullpen. I had come up as a reliever, and I felt that among the rest of the pitchers on the staff, I would be the one who could help the team the most out there. Also, I had proved I could be a starter and win. This would be the chance for me to see for myself whether I could also make it as a reliever.

There was another reason I wanted to go into the bullpen. With Goose out, Lem was using Tidrow, who pitched best in long relief, as the short relief man, and Dick was having difficulty getting untracked. I was Dick's roommate on the road and a neighbor of his at home during the season, and I shared his agony. I knew if I could fill Goose's role, Dick could return to do what he does best.

Lem and George Steinbrenner finally agreed to let me give it a try, and against the Oakland A's I relieved Catfish with one out in the seventh and a man on third, and I struck out the first batter and got the second one to pop out. In all I pitched three and two-thirds innings and we won when Jim Spencer hit a home run in the tenth. I had forgotten how much fun it could be to pitch relief. I was credited with a second save before I returned to the starting rotation.

I had considered the effect on me physically prior to volunteering for relief duty but I never considered the public reaction to my offering. It was too much. I don't feel I'm unique among athletes. I believe the majority of us are not concerned about our own stats, runs batted in, and strikeouts recorded as much as we are concerned about the good of the team and the other players. I feel my teammates made me what I was in 1978; it was my way of returning the favor. I didn't listen to the prophets of doom who were predicting that my left arm was going to fall off or that one morning I would wake up and find out I couldn't lift a cup of coffee.

There were also some personal reasons for my going to the bullpen. I had made my way to the big leagues as a reliever but had never established myself as a success in that area. I wanted to prove to myself that I could have made it as a reliever. Also, I wanted to free myself from the burden of answering questions comparing 1979 to 1978. I had said all along that comparison was impossible but no one seemed to be listening. And when I didn't start out as fast, some reporters were predicting I had lost it all. By going to the bullpen, I halted all comparison of this season to last season. There was no way I could win twenty-five games spending all that time in the bullpen.

My pitching relief also saved Dick for a while, but then Lem ended up overpitching him. He called on Dick to pitch on a Friday night, then a Saturday, and then a Sunday against the California Angels, and each time Dick halted a rally. In that Sunday game he came into the game in the seventh and got out of a jam, and then it rained, and the game was held up for thirty-five minutes.

Dick told Lem his arm was tightening up and that it would be wise to bring in another pitcher when the game resumed, but Bob, figuring he had no one else, asked Dick to stick it out. Dick agreed, but he told Lem that if the first two runners got on, he'd want to come out. Lem agreed.

Well, the first two batters got on, but when he looked toward the dugout, Lem had disappeared. The next five batters got hits. Then Lem took him out.

I never saw Dick so angry. He stormed into the locker room, swearing at his embarrassment, and he demanded a meeting with the front office. When George Steinbrenner heard of Tidrow's outburst and demand, he ordered Al Rosen to trade him. Rosen, faced with no choice, sent Dick to Chicago for Ray Burris, who was gone at the end of the season. Dick went to the Cubs and performed as we all knew he would. When the Cubs' Bruce Sutter won the Cy Young Award this year, he credited Dick's help in enabling him to win the award. Tidrow became the middle relief man that Chicago and Sutter so badly needed. Unfortunately, however, for the Yankees, when I went back to a starting role, the team continued to play mediocre baseball, and I was really down because at the All-Star break my record was only 6–7. I was probably pitching as good as ever, but we weren't scoring many runs, and it was frustrating.

In the last game I pitched before the All-Star game I had a one-run lead going into the ninth against the California Angels, but Bobby Grich hit a two-run homer in the bottom of the ninth and we got beat. And it got worse. Lem picked me for the All-Star game, based on my '78 season I'm sure, and Bonnie and Jamie flew in to Los Angeles to meet me for our flight to the All-Star game in Seattle. When we got in, we went to the airline counter for our tickets, but there were no tickets. They were being held at another airline, what seemed like a mile away. We flew to Seattle, and we rented a car to take us to the ballpark, and on the way the car broke down. I was getting a hint about this game, and I should have taken the hint. In the ninth inning Lem called me in to relieve. The score was tied and the bases were loaded, and Lee Mazzilli of the Mets was the batter. What did I do? I walked Mazzilli, forcing in the winning run. Big-shot 25–3 pitcher in front of millions of people on national TV!

The next day I called my friend, attorney and agent, John Schneider. My state of mind was terrible, and I sorely needed someone to talk to, so sorely in fact that I had him fly up to New York.

I was telling him how down I felt, and he said, "Ronnie, you've hit rock bottom. You probably feel as low as you're ever going to feel in your life. Things can't be worse." Then he said, "I just want to ask you one thing. Do you still believe you're one of the best pitchers in baseball?"

I said, "Yes, I do."

And John said, "If you ever start feeling anything different, I'll kick your ass all the way back to Louisiana."

I laughed. And the rest of the season I went out and really pitched well and finished up by winning 13 of my last 15.

It would have been a most satisfying year, finishing 18–8, except for one major occurrence: the death of Thurman Munson. When I'm out there on the pitcher's mound, I see myself as a general, and after I began pitching for the Yankees I came to understeand that Thurman was also a general, someone who had such great knowledge of the hitters that I could rely on him completely. I could forget about calling the ballgame and just throw what he wanted me to throw. Thurman was an important factor in my pitching success.

It was a dark, gloomy afternoon the day he died. Bonnie and her mom and dad and I were sitting in our home in New Jersey when the phone rang. It was George Steinbrenner. George said, "Ronnie, Thurman's dead. He crashed his plane." My mind started to spin. I

131

went over and turned down the sound of the television set and sat in my rocking chair and rocked for the next five hours without saying a word.

He died on Thursday, August 2, and he was buried on Monday, the same day I was scheduled to pitch against Baltimore on national TV, and when I went out to the mound for the first inning, I looked toward home plate, and I just could not believe that Thurman would not be there ever again.

We were losing the game 4–1 in the seventh inning, and Billy came to take me out, but I told him, "I may lose this ballgame, but I'm not going to come out until it's over. I *have* to win this one. This one's for Thurman." And Billy understood, so he left me in. In the bottom of the inning, Bobby Murcer hit a two-run home run. Then in the bottom of the ninth, he drove in two more runs, and we won the game 5–4. Murcer and Thurman were close, and winning that game meant a lot to him, too. In fact, it meant a lot to all of us.

I was winning consistently now, but after Thurman died, it was more difficult than before. When Thurman was there, I never questioned whether he was calling for the right pitch. However, with the young catchers back there, sometimes they would call for a pitch that I didn't feel was right, and then I was faced with a dilemma. Do I throw a pitch I don't want to throw, or do I shake the catcher off and perhaps undermine his confidence? Usually I chose to throw the pitch called for, and more often than not the batter would hit it, because I wasn't throwing a pitch I wanted to throw. I found myself second-guessing my catcher too often, and again, I was winning—the team was hitting much better in the second half—but they were not easy wins.

I could have won 20 games, as it turned out. Catfish was pitching late in the season, and he had a big lead in the fourth inning when he injured himself. Billy offered to let me go in, pitch an inning and pick up a gift win, but I felt that Ron Davis, a rookie who had won 12 games, would benefit more from the win, so I let him go in and win it. Then in my final start of the season I needed three strikeouts to total 200 for the season, making me the first Yankee ever to do that two years in a row, and in that game I got four strikeouts in three innings, and we had a lead. Another win would have given Davis the record for wins for a rookie reliever, so I told Billy to send him in, and he did, and Davis won the game, and no one was happier about it than I was. My longest season was finally over.

I still can't believe Thurman's not with us anymore. I remember after Mike Caldwell beat me in 1978 to stop my winning streak. Just before Billy came out to yank me, Thurman came out to the mound. He said, "Gid, for the last hour I've been watching those clouds in deep center field. They form, and then suddenly they break up, only to re-form a few minutes later." Billy interrupted us at that point, and as I walked toward the dugout I was wondering what Thurman was talking about.

Now, however, I know. He was telling me that whatever happens, life goes on, win or lose, with or without Thurman Munson, or for that matter, Ron Guidry. We can't take life, baseball, or ourselves, too seriously.

8

The Brother I Always Wanted

I always wanted a younger brother. Someone to share time with. Someone to teach the art of hunting to. For seventeen years I was an only child, and I'd pretty much given up hope, then one day I came home from high school and my momma said, "Ronnie, guess what? I'm pregnant."

I couldn't believe it. All these years I had been hoping it would happen. I started hollering and running around the house, and I called Boo Menard and said, "We're gonna celebrate tonight," and we bought a couple of six packs of beer and really tied one on. The next day at school I told everyone I knew. The whole school knew that my mom was pregnant and that I was going to be a brother. I have the greatest friends, and because they knew what this meant to me, everyone was happy for me, and every day at school someone would say, "How's your mom? How is she feeling?" and everything was going fine.

I was making plans as the birth date approached. I packed a suitcase for my mom and put it by the door, and I rehearsed my route in case I had to rush her to the hospital. I knew just what roads to take, and one time I drove it real slow, in case there was no hurry, and one time I practiced it real fast, running all the lights, just to see how long it would take. Made it in less than fifteen minutes, in fact. I told Momma, "Don't you worry if it comes all of a sudden. I've got the situation under control."

I always thought getting ready for the trip to the hospital was kind of silly, something they do on TV, like when the husband would rush off to the hospital leaving the wife behind, or he'd forget the suitcase or get lost. But when it was my mother, I didn't think it was silly anymore. This was serious business.

One day when I got home Momma wasn't feeling well. "I'm having pains," she said. My dad and I weren't going to take any chances. We piled into the car, and as we were going to the hospital, I was thinking, "Ronnie, try to act cool and calm," but when I looked down at my hands, they were shaking, and I couldn't control myself. Over and over I kept whispering to myself, "Christ, let's hurry, let's get there and make sure nothing happens."

The nurses took Momma into the delivery room, and Dad and I waited outside. I never drank so many sodas in my life. The waiting room was barren except for the Coke machine, and I was so nervous I went to it every five minutes.

"What do you hope it is?" my father asked.

I didn't tell him how I really felt, but I was actually hoping for a boy. Mom had somehow known that, because several days earlier she had asked me, "What are you going to name your brother?" and I told her "Conrad" after the St. Louis Cardinal football player Bobby Conrad. Mom said, "Anything you like, I like." However, just before it was time to go to the hospital, I changed my mind. I decided I wanted to name him Travis after Travis Williams, the star running back of the Green Bay Packers. I told my father he could name it if it turned out to be a girl.

After what seemed an eternity, a nurse appeared holding a tiny baby. I could tell right away it had a lot of dark hair. Before I could ask, "What is it?" she said, "It's a boy."

I wanted to jump and scream and holler, but then the doctor came in, and he had a serious look on his face, a look that bothered me. He told Dad, "Your wife had a little trouble."

"What do you mean?" Dad asked, and he and the doctor walked away to talk. They wheeled Momma into her private room, where we were waiting, and when they brought her in I could see that she had been sedated and that she had had a rough time. When she passed by, she said, "Roland, there's something wrong."

Dad tried to comfort her. "Don't worry, Grace, everything's fine," he said. "Nothing's wrong." I desperately wanted to believe him but deep in my heart I knew something *was* wrong.

Mom and Dad wanted to spend some time alone, so I asked one of the nurses to take me to see Travis. The nurse was squeezing him, turning him over kind of roughly, and I yelled at her, but she laughed and told me not to worry, that she knew what she was doing.

When Dad came out, I asked him what had happened. "Mom had complications delivering the baby," he said.

"Mom said something was wrong. What was it?"

"Something went wrong when she gave birth," he said. "That's all I know."

"You sure?" I asked, desperately wanting to hear something different.

"I'm sure," he said.

I went to school the next day with a big smile on my face. I had a group of about ten to fifteen kids I hung around with, and when I walked into the gym in the morning, I said real loud, "I'm a brother," and as I said it, it echoed throughout the gym, and everyone heard and cheered. A couple of my friends asked if they could go to the hospital to see him, and I asked Dad and he said sure, and that afternoon there was bedlam at the hospital when more than a hundred of my classmates showed up.

During the eight days Travis stayed in the hospital, nothing appeared to be wrong. My parents hadn't told me that when he was born he almost didn't make it. After Momma brought him home, as soon as I got back from school I would go into his room just to look at him and touch him. He was a beautiful baby, with his tiny little hands and feet, and it took me another week to notice something: Travis didn't cry, something I had thought all babies did.

I came home early from school one day and when I walked inside there was Dad sitting at the kitchen table with his head in his hands, crying. "Oh God," I thought, "something's happened," and with my heart pounding as I walked over to him I prayed nothing serious had happened. I put my hand on his shoulder. "Daddy, what's wrong?" I said. "What is it that can make you cry?"

"I just wanted to get something off my chest," he said.

"It must weigh a ton," I said.

"We got a call from the doctor," he said. "He wants us to bring Travis in for some tests. He thinks there's something physically and mentally wrong with him."

"Is that why he doesn't cry?" I asked. "He's never made a sound. Will he be deaf and dumb?"

Dad looked up at me grimly. "I'll let you know as soon as I find out," he said.

What we found out was that Travis was brain-damaged from birth.

When I returned to school, everyone noticed a change in me. I wasn't the same. I wasn't avoiding anyone; I just didn't feel like talking. When anyone would ask about Travis, I'd just say, "He's okay," and leave it at that. The only person I told was Boo, and when I told him, he cried.

The other students started saying, "I wonder what's the matter with Gid?" and gradually word got out that Travis was retarded, or handicapped or whatever—there's really no good word for it—and they'd come over and try to cheer me up. They'd come over to my house to see him and to say hello to my parents.

Travis was about four weeks old when I came home and saw Momma and Dad smiling for the first time since he was born. "What's goin' on?" I asked. She said, "Just be patient and you'll find out," and that's all she said. I was watching TV in the living room, and from Travis's bedroom I heard him. He was crying. I listened, and I ran into his room when I heard it, and sure enough, Travis was crying, and all of a sudden I

139

started crying uncontrollably. I hadn't cried like that since I was a baby myself. I cried so much I couldn't see for an hour.

As he grew older Travis began making more and more sounds, and I was hoping that Travis would grow up and be like a normal child, but Dad would bring me back to reality. "Don't be surprised if it takes Travis two years to walk," he would say. "We don't know how bad it is."

It made me angry. "I'm not going to wait that long to see him walk," I said. "I'll make him walk before then." And I would always play with him like he was normal. Momma would say, "Ronald, don't forget Travis is handicapped," and I'd see red. "I'll make him handicapped," I'd yell. "I'll break both his legs. By the time I'm finished with him, he's going to walk, he's going to run, and he's going to throw." And I played with him. I played rough with him. Daddy and I would exercise his muscles for hours. We'd get him to laugh, and he started becoming much more normal than the doctors expected him to be. I'd bring him into bed with me and play games with him and talk to him, and finally, he would drop off to sleep.

Travis always had a lot of trouble getting to sleep. When he was a week old and still in the hospital, he would never sleep. One time when Dad went to see him, he put a pillow on his lap and took Travis out of the crib and laid him on the pillow, and Dad talked to him and rubbed his little back, and before long Travis fell asleep.

When the nurse came in, she saw Travis out of his crib and she became alarmed. "Mr. Guidry," she said, "what are you doing? He's not supposed to be out of bed."

"Well, he's sleeping, isn't he," Dad said. "I got him to sleep."

The nurse calmed down. "He is sleeping," she said. "It's the first time I've seen him sleep. What did you do?"

He told her. Travis slept for three hours that day, and every time Daddy tried to put him back into his crib, he'd wake up. So long as Dad would hold him, he'd sleep.

As Travis got a little older, his handicaps became more noticeable. He didn't have much coordination, and he had trouble controlling one of his legs, so he wasn't able to walk until he was between two and three years old. We worked for months with Travis, taking one leg and putting it in front of the other one, and always holding him so he wouldn't fall. One day at my cousins' house, we turned him loose, and cousin Mike got ready to catch Travis when he fell, but he didn't fall. He wobbled a couple of steps, and Mike's eyes got real big, and he started calling for everyone to come into the room, and when we got there we all started cheering.

He didn't talk until he was four years old. He made sounds before then, but he could never pronounce words. He still has trouble pronouncing them; it's hard to understand what he's saying if you haven't been around him for a while.

He was out riding with Mom and Dad when he actually spoke a word. Dad would try to show Travis which way to go, and when they would come to a familiar road, Dad would say, "Which way?" and Travis would point. Travis loves to give directions, just like I did when I took my old aunts. Anyway, on this day Travis made a special sign that indicated he wanted to drive to Grandpa Gus's. Dad figured that Travis had already made some sounds and he'd already cried, and if he could do that, he could say words, and so he kept after him. Dad said to Travis, "If you don't say 'Grandpa' we're not going." Travis didn't try. Dad tried another way. He said, "Okay. Try to say 'Gus,'" figuring it would be easier to say. "You want to see Pop Gus?" He grunted. "Then say 'Gus' and we'll go," Dad said. "Say 'Gus.'" And Travis said "Gus." Ordinarily Cajuns do not call their grandparents by their first names, but Dad told Momma, "If he can say 'Gus' your dad will be so

141

happy. He won't mind." When they got to Gus's house, he wasn't there, but when they called him later that afternoon to tell him about it, Gus got out of bed and drove fifteen miles to hear Travis say his name.

Once Gus took Travis out for a ride, and as they were driving Travis pointed left. He turned left. "Where do you want to go?" Gus asked. He kept driving, and Travis pointed right. Gus went right. He kept driving, and suddenly Travis yelled out, "There," and when Gus looked it was the local ice-cream parlor.

Soon afterward Travis started saying a lot of things. Since I went to college in my hometown, after school I would come home, and often I would practice my drums. I'd get Travis and set him up on a stool and give him a stick and ask him to play the soul music with me. It was fun for him, and it also helped the coordination with his arms. One afternoon I came home and said, "Hi, Travis," and he said, "Soul," and I did a double-take. It took me a while to figure out that he was associating soul music with me, and so his name for me was "Soul." He calls me Soul to this day.

The only time he called me something else was a brief period when Bonnie and I were living at my parents' home and I was in the habit of saying "Alright" when I got excited about something and Travis started calling me "Alright." Bonnie often used "Okay" and he would call her "Okay."

We knew we were going to have to be patient with Travis. He couldn't say, "Momma, I want some water," but he did learn to say "water." He couldn't say, "I'd like to eat," but he did learn "eat," which was good enough for us. We worked with him and supported him and encouraged him, but we didn't push him, because we knew it would take time and we had all the time in the world.

You learn to appreciate the little triumphs when you work with a handicapped child. By normal standards, it may be nothing at all, but for a handicapped child, it seems monumental. It must be put in perspective.

When Travis was about seven he started drawing and coloring in school, and he'd bring his work home, and you had no idea what it was he was drawing, but he was the proudest little kid in the whole world, and we were just as proud. I'd come home, and the first thing he'd say would be, "Look, Soul, Mama," and he'd show me a picture of a big X, and I'd hug him and tell him how terrific it was.

One thing he's real proud of is his ability to put puzzles together. He loves them. He must have a couple dozen of them, each one with ten or fifteen big pieces, and he could fit them together like it was nothing. I happen to stink at putting puzzles together. We'd be sitting on the floor working on one of his puzzles, and I'd put a piece in, and he'd say, "No, Soul," and he'd take the piece out and put it where it belonged. A lot of times my friend Bobby and I will try to put together one of his puzzles, and we'll spend five minutes trying to figure out where one piece goes, and Travis will watch us and shake his head and walk away. Momma will say, "Travis, show them where it goes," and he'll come over and in two seconds put it where it belongs.

Like with everyone else, with handicapped children the effort counts more than anything. I've made several appearances for the Special Olympics program, and what I tell the kids is that if you're going to be an athlete, you have to give a hundred percent. If that means throwing a ball five feet, then throw it five feet, and that'll be tremendous. Not trying is what I can't condone. That's the attitude I've always had with Travis. I don't pamper him, and I still play rough with him, show him new things.

We'd go outside and play football, and I'd show him how to hold the ball, and then tell him, "Now look, run over there, run fast, because I'm going to try to catch you," and he'd take off, and I'd urge him on and I'd say, "Oh, you're too fast, let me try again." And we'd do it again and again, and finally after he'd got in some good running, I'd catch him and hold him and we'd tumble to the ground together. Today when I see him I'll say, "Ready, down, set, take off," and he'll get down in a three-point stance and run off, and I'll run after him and catch him.

Hide-and-seek was another game we played a lot. We'd do it in the house, and he hated it when I hid in the closet. He'd get scared, because he'd open the door and I'd jump out at him, and he'd take off. He'd never go into the closet himself. His favorite spot was the side of the bed. He'd curl up on the floor beside the bed and close his eyes, figuring that if he couldn't see me, then I couldn't see him. I'd get down and crawl around the floor and say, "I wonder where Travis is?" and he'd love that, hiding there, not able to be seen in his own mind.

Because Travis has complete faith that I would never let anything happen to him, he's willing to try something even when he's afraid.

During the winter I hunt almost every day, and when I return he'll ask me, "Where you been?" I'll say, "I've been hunting," and I'll show him the birds or rabbits or whatever I caught. One day I showed him my gun and asked if he wanted to learn how to shoot it. "*Mmmmmmmm,*" is what he said. I said, "Why don't you come walk with me back by the canal and watch how I do it?" He nodded. We went behind the house to the canal, and he threw things into the water and watched the splash. I threw a bottle into the water, and as it floated there, I took a shot at it, and he watched it shatter. Travis grabbed my pants. He was scared by the noise.

"It won't hurt you, Travis. Nothing's gonna happen. Here, watch, I'll do it again, and nothing will happen." I shot another bottle.

"Oh," was all he said.

That day I shot about ten times, just enough to get him a little used to the sound. I didn't want to overdo it.

The next day I said, "I'm going back to the canal. Want to come?" He hesitated. I started to go. He ran after me. This day I shot about twenty shells, and after a while he'd come with me when I went hunting, and he'd sit and watch all day while I hunted.

One day when we were out in the woods I asked him if he wanted to take a shot. He nodded. But when I gave him the gun, he backed away from it. I said, "Look, Travis, I won't let anything hurt you. Don't be afraid." I stood behind him and grabbed ahold of him real tight with my right arm to give him security, and with my left arm I held the gun up in a shooting position for him. I said, "Just give me your finger, and we'll pull the trigger." He tensed, but he didn't try to run off. He put his finger to the trigger and pulled it. He got scared again when it went off and quickly handed the gun back to me. I took a shot, and again I told him it wouldn't hurt us. He took it again, and again I wrapped my arms around him, and he fired. After the shot went off, he looked at me and smiled. In all, he fired about six times, and by the end of the day he had overcome his fear. Each time he'd fired into the water, and when the bullet would make a big splash, he'd get all excited and laugh, and I'd laugh. I felt good that he had overcome his fear and was enjoying a new experience.

The worst thing you can do to a child, any child, but especially a handicapped child, is to shelter him so that you're stopping him from learning and doing things on his own. You can't always be doing things for the child, because all that does is instill a lack of self-confidence and a fear of the world around him. You've got to talk to him and listen to him and consult him and always make him feel a part of your world, but the steps he takes must be his own.

Travis loves baseball. Momma tells me that whenever I'm pitching on TV, he sits glued to the set the whole game. Though he doesn't really understand what's going on, he knows that it's Soul on TV, and that's all that matters. He has reached the point where he knows a lot of the players. If I say to him, "Who's number 30?" he won't say Willie Randolph, but if you ask him who plays second base, then he will. Dent, Nettles, he knows them. The only problem he has is with the outfield. He doesn't know the positions left field and right field, but when I asked him, "Travis, who's by the pole?" he'll say Roy White. If I ask him, "Who's by the foul line?" he'll say Reggie Jackson. The funny thing is, when I ask him, "Who's your favorite Yankee?" he'll say "Catfish Hunter." I'm not even sure why. Sometimes he'll say Reggie's his favorite, and once in a long while he'll say "Soul." Now that Catfish is retired, I'll have a better chance.

Travis doesn't play ball yet, because he doesn't have much coordination in his hands, but he has dreams about playing. He's got some imagination. He's in his own little world. One day my dad picked him up from school, and as soon as he got into the car, Travis folded his arms and sat up straight, a position he assumes when he wants to be very serious. He said, "I'm on the ball team."

Daddy said, "Oh yeah?"

He said, "Yep." Travis has a funny way of saying yep.

"What position do you play?" Dad asked him.

"Shortstop."

"Are you good?"

"Yep."

"Do you bat?"

"Yep."

"What do you hit?" Travis didn't understand what he meant and looked puzzled. "Do you hit singles or doubles or triples or home runs?"

Travis said, "Triples." The next day Dad went to school, and he asked one of the teachers if Travis was really on the team. He wasn't. He had made the whole thing up.

Once Momma was cooking dinner, and Travis went

over to my dad, who was outside, and he said, "Momma said to go to the store to get some mustard greens." Dad went inside and asked Momma if she had said that. She hadn't. He just imagined it, because that's what he wanted to eat. Dad and Travis got in the car and they drove to the store and bought mustard greens.

Travis's mind never stops working, and he's made tremendous progress. It wasn't too long ago that we thought he'd never speak in full sentences, and now he does it all the time, and it seems that every time I see him he's learned to do something new. It might be making a puzzle or making a drawing or saying a word, whatever; all that matters is that he's growing. He's always surprising me, and a lot of other people too.

One time my father and Travis went into a store and there were five men in there talking baseball. They were trying to remember the name of the pitcher who the Yankees lost to the Red Sox in the 1978 free-agent draft. When my dad walked in, one of them said, "Here's Mr. Guidry. He'll know the guy's name." They asked him, and they were waiting for an answer, and my dad said, "Wait a minute. Let me ask Travis." The men kind of chuckled. They knew Travis, and they didn't think there was any way he would know. Dad asked him, "Who was the pitcher who won two games in the World Series?" Travis quickly said, "Mike Torrez." My dad said, "Thank you, Travis," and they walked out, leaving the men with their mouths open.

Another time my dad and Travis were at the train station. Travis goes with my dad quite a lot, and he's gotten to know that when a yellow signal flashes it means a train is approaching and when it flashes red, it's about to pull into the station. He can also tell the difference between the whistle of a passenger train and that of a freight train.

They were standing there at the station, and Travis took it upon himself to notify the crew in the station house when the red signal was flashing. He'd often yell out, "In the red. Time to go," and get all excited. Well, this one day he shouted out that the train was coming, and the people in the waiting room started to go outside. Travis himself ran outside, and before anyone could see the train, the whistle blew, and Travis said, "Oh oh, it's a freight train." A few seconds later the train appeared, and sure enough it was a freight train. A lady who had been standing nearby had been waiting for about an hour, and she'd noticed him and realized his situation, and she looked at my father and said, "How did he know? He's like he is, and he knows the difference between the trains."

My daddy just smiled at her. "Yeah, he knows," he said.

Travis is one of the most contented children I've ever seen. He's rarely cross, and he looks forward to going to school because he loves to be with the other kids. Competition doesn't mean anything to him. Travis enters the Special Olympics down here in Lafayette, and he's done pretty well in the softball throw, for instance, but what gets me is that even though he's far and away the fastest kid in his group, he has never once won a race. When the race starts, he'll dash out to a ten-yard lead every time, and he'll stay way out in front until he's about ten yards from the finish line. Then he'll stop and wave to everyone else, telling them to hurry and catch up. When everybody has passed him, he'll then cross the finish line. For three years now he has done this. As I said, he doesn't care about winning. He feels so close to the other kids that after he runs far out in front of them, he feels bad and wants to be with them. Come to think of it, it makes more sense than anyone has ever given him credit for having.

I can't spend as much time with Travis as I used to, what with our moving into our own house and with my being busy during the baseball season, but the physical distance hasn't made us any less close. He'll never know how much joy he brings into my life. As yet, much as I try to accept him the way he is, I find it difficult.

I know that Travis might never be half of what a normal child is, but I look at myself and say, "Well, I'm his brother. We both have the same mom and dad, and yet I'm perfectly normal and he's not. I've been able to attain national recognition and he'll never get that chance. I've been able to do everything in the world, and he won't. Why am I here on earth having such a good time while he can't? I tell myself that he has to be here for a reason. Often I ask myself, "Does God intend to show us what love is? Because with a child like this it is impossible to shower him with enough love." My mom and dad have so much love for him, I respect them even more than before. It would be so easy for them to say, "Let's put him in a home." It doesn't seem right that they have to work so hard for him. All my mom does from eight in the morning until five in the afternoon is sit outside and watch him play. The only time she gets up is when she's hungry or if she has to answer the phone. Can you imagine doing that every day? And yet she does. So when sometimes something doesn't work out for me, I may gripe, but then I think about my mom, and I think, "There's meaning in this somewhere." I ask God *why* a lot in my prayers. I ask Him, "Are You going to show me much later why this is, or am I so dense I cannot look it in the eye and say, 'This is why'?" I exhaust myself thinking about it.

To my parents it's simply God's way, and in their eyes they are twice blessed to have a Ronnie and a Travis to bring love and meaning into their lives. I know they are proud of me, but the beautiful thing is that they are just as proud of Travis.

When Travis was an infant, a family friend gave my parents a poem. It expresses the way they feel about Travis better than anything I could say. It's up on their kitchen wall. The poem is called "Heaven's Very Special Child":

A meeting was held quite far from earth,
"It's time again for another birth,"
Said the angels to the Lord above.
"This special child will need much love."
His progress may seem very slow,
Accomplishment he may not show;
And he'll require extra care
From the folks he meets down there.

He may not run or laugh or play,
His thoughts may seem quite far away.
In many ways he won't accept,
And he'll be known as handicapped.
So let's be careful where he's sent,
We want his life to be content.
Please, Lord, find the parents who
Will do a special job for you.

They will not realize right away,
The leading part they're asked to play.
But with this child sent from above
Comes stronger faith and richer love.
And soon they'll know the privilege given
In caring for this gift from Heaven.
This precious charge, so meek and mild
Is Heaven's Very Special Child.

After the 1978 season, I was given the Victor Award for significant achievement. The award ceremony was at Yankee Stadium on national TV, and when I got to the microphone to accept the award, I said, "I'd like to thank the people who made this honor possible. I'm very happy to receive it, but I must say, I'm not as happy as I was when I heard that my little brother Travis won second place in the Special Olympics softball throw competition."

I'd trade every significant achievement I've ever made to see Travis continue to progress and be able to lead a reasonably normal life. He's the one who has made the truly significant achievements. He's come a long, long way, but no matter what he does or how far he progresses, he'll always mean something to me that no one else ever can. In his own way, he has shown me what it is to need love and to be loved, and, like the poem says, he has given me stronger faith and richer love. He is, indeed, a very special child. He's the little brother I always wanted.

9

Everything Remains the Same

During the war years, when my parents were growing up, there was little time for recreation. You didn't drive downtown to the supermarket to do the grocery shopping because there was no supermarket, no downtown, and no car to drive. Cajuns had to hunt and farm their own food. Everyone had chickens and turkeys in their backyard. The chickens would provide eggs, and vegetables would come from the garden planted out back. Two big chunks of ice, delivered each week by the iceman, preserved foods that otherwise would have gone bad.

Many farmers had cattle, and you couldn't work the cattle on foot, so a good riding horse was a must, and everyone in the family would use it. When work was done for the day and you wanted to take a girl to the local dance, you'd ask your parents if you could use the horse. The girl's parents would bring her to the dance in a wagon, and they'd wait there with her, and when the dance was over, they'd take her home, and you'd ride back home on your horse. It was a simple life, a private life, yet often just the act of getting food brought people together.

Because there wasn't any refrigeration, neighbors had to share with other neighbors. Each week or so one of the neighbors had the responsibility of providing everyone with beef or pork. Farmers kept their hogs in pens until the animals weighed about five hundred pounds. The day the animal was to be killed, everyone would get up early in the morning, and the youngsters would gather wood for the fire, piling it up next to the large, black kettle. The man responsible for killing the hog was called the boucherie. He was the local butcher. You brought him your cow or pig and he would cut it up for you.

Nothing was wasted. A hog provided meat, bacon, and lard, which was used instead of butter or cooking oil. One hog could produce thirty to forty pounds of lard. That was kept by the owner of the hog.

The ladies would clean out the hog's intestines, which were used to make a Cajun delicacy called boudin, which is hot and spicy and tastes like sausage.

Back then the staple crop was rice. Levees made out of dirt had to be built so that water could flood the land and allow the rice to grow. Then as the water would lie there, the crawfish would make their way onto your land, and when it was time to let the water out, the farmers would take deep sacks and put them in the cuts of the levees. They'd catch thousands of crawfish and afterward they'd have a crawfish festival. Pretty soon crawfish became more valuable than rice, and some farmers began cultivating the crawfish as a way to make a living.

While lobster is found off the east coast of the United States, in the Atlantic Ocean, and normally range in size larger than twelve inches, the crawfish is more frequently found in the rice paddies and rarely are larger than three inches.

You have not eaten good food until you have enjoyed a true crawfish dinner comprised of crawfish étouffée, fried crawfish tails, and boiled crawfish, crawfish au gratin, crawfish pie, and bell pepper stuffed with crawfish. A crawfish salad is also offered as an appetizer.

Every May of an even year—for example, 1980—Breaux Bridge, the self-proclaimed Crawfish Capital of the World, hosts the Crawfish Festival and over a hundred thousand people flock to this small town of only a couple thousand to let the good times roll. Laissez les bons temps rouler!

In the bayou country no one ever went hungry because there was always the woods for hunting. Anytime a person wanted, he could go out with the family shotgun and bring home a couple of ducks or other birds or a rabbit, and there would be food on the table. It was a tough life, but it was a good life. Cajuns never did have a great need for money and material wealth. We have the woods and our family and our friends, and that's more than most people have.

By the time I was a kid, indoor plumbing and electricity and the telephone had come to Lafayette, but it was still a small town. You couldn't go anywhere without running into somebody you knew. The town was easy to get around, we could bicycle anywhere we wanted, and we could hunt just about anywhere we wanted. All we had to do was ask permission of the landowner. Or if we wanted to go out into the marshes, it was just a matter of driving your car to the banks, taking your boat down to the shore, and putting it into the water at a convenient spot. It was open territory, and no one bothered you.

Now things are changing. The big oil companies have bought up or leased the best tracts of marsh for duck hunting. At first when they bought the land they didn't care whether people used it or not, but after they lived here awhile and saw how important it was to be able to hunt, they began putting signs on their land keeping everyone off. Other than a few places where the owners have refused to sell out, the best duck-hunting land is private, and you have to be someone special to hunt on it.

Because of my pitching success I've been offered opportunities to hunt on private land. I tell them the same thing every time I am asked, that if I go, they must let me bring Grandpa Gus or someone else. If I can't hunt with my family and friends, then I don't want to go.

After my 25-3 season I was offered a membership in a national hunting club. They have tracts all over the country, and I would have been able to go for free anytime I wanted. Under their rules, however, I could bring a friend only one time to each lease, and after going five times, the friend was no longer welcome.

When I was offered membership I called Bobby Badeaux on the phone and asked his advice as to whether I should join. The club is a prestigious organization, and it was an opportunity to meet influential people, a chance to hunt with a lot of big wheels. I said to Bobby, "I need your help. Should I join?" Bobby said, "For me, the most important thing about hunting is me and you being together. We share something when we hunt. We laugh at dumb shots, congratulate each other on good ones. Telling you, 'Dumb ass, why did you scare away the bird I was about to shoot,' is more fun than shooting it." He said, "If I couldn't hunt with you, you can take my shotgun away and give it to the Salvation Army."

I said, "Bobby, I feel the same way, and I'll always feel the same way," and when it came time to decide whether or not to join, I respectfully declined.

After that 1978 season, I was so looking forward to coming home and being with my family and friends. I was afraid that my success was going to change things, and I guess my friends were probably afraid of the same thing. I valued their friendship and, wanting them to know how much, when I got home I called them and invited them over to tell them that we would be friends forever. That means more to me than twenty-five wins and the money I earned that season. For Cajuns, friends will always be more important than money.

As a kid, I had just as much fun with no money as I did when I had a dollar, and it would be just as true today. If Daddy gave me some money, it went a long way before it was spent, because I saw how he earned it, how hard my grandfather had to work to earn it, and I was going to make sure I didn't spend it foolishly.

Sometimes on Saturday and Sunday I would work with my dad doing carpentry work. I'd work an eight-hour day and make five dollars. It was seventy-five cents an hour, and it was well-earned, and you can bet that if I had five dollars it went a long way before it was spent.

When I was young and I was given money, I used to dig holes in my backyard and bury it. I had a secret compartment in the back of my rabbit cage. I cut a little square in the back of the cage with a razor blade, and when I got change, I dropped the nickels and dimes and quarters in that cage just as though it was a bank. I did this for about seven years, and when I was about thirteen my parents moved to where they live now, and I almost forgot about it. For a couple of weeks before we were set to move I had been saying to myself, "Don't forget about the money in the cage," and on the day we moved, I kissed my grandmother good-bye and went back to the cage and removed a couple of boards in the back of the cage. The coins flew everywhere. They just poured out. There must have been a hundred dollars worth of change. And I took that money and put it in the bank. I wanted the interest. When you're twelve years old, if you make a dime on a dollar, that's a lot of money.

I've understood what money can do to people since I was a little kid. The oil people have always been around Lafayette. My daddy heard of them when he was growing up around here. Nevertheless, it wasn't until the 1950's that they took offices in the city, and when that happened the town boomed overnight.

The way Lafayette is divided, the sons of the oil executives, the doctors, and the lawyers went to Lafayette High School on the south side of town. The Cajun boys mostly went to North Side High School. We wore blue jeans with patches and walked to school. They wore nice slacks and nice shoes and drove cars.

And every year when our North Side teams would play them in the park, or if we played them in Legion ball, we would win, and it would give us a great deal of satisfaction.

I suppose I could have made a great deal more money than I have, but it wouldn't have been my way of doing things.

I had played Legion ball with a Lafayette boy by the name of John Schneider, and after my first good season with the Yankees, the town of Lafayette wanted to throw a little party for me. Schneider who became a councilman and an attorney, coordinated the affair, and after it was over I called him on the phone and asked him if he would represent me in my contract negotiations with the Yankees. He did, and he did an excellent job. The next year was the 25–3 year, and during the season, John called me and said, "Ronnie, I'm just a small-town boy from Lafayette. The William Morris Agency has called me and told me they are interested in handling you." John said, "In my opinion they have the potential to make money for you that I don't have. They have connections I don't. For your own good I think you should talk with them."

I called the agency, and I was rather impressed. I then called John and asked him, "If I went with William Morris, what would you do?" He said, "There wouldn't be much left for me to do." I said, "John, I'd hate to see you unemployed. I think I'm going to stick with you." He was my friend, and I trusted him implicitly, and that was good enough for me.

When I swallowed my tobacco, in a game early in the 1978 season it gave me nationwide attention, and I was soon contacted by a chewing tobacco company to do a commercial. John figured the money was good and knew that I chewed tobacco, but when he told me about the offer, I turned it down flat. I told him, "I chew it because it keeps me alert and awake on the mound. However, I really don't want to encourage kids to start chewing tobacco. I don't want to be that kind of influence," and I turned it down flat.

The next commercial offered me was from a soft-drink concern. The Uncola. John called me, all excited, and told me about the offer, and I told him, "John, I drink Dr Pepper. I've drunk Dr Pepper since I was a kid and I won't endorse any product I don't use myself. Also," I said, "I won't endorse any product I would not use in the future." That submarined my second offer.

Then a group of East Coast Oldsmobile dealers

wanted me to represent them. They offered me $30,000 to do a one-shot TV commercial. I told John, "I have nothing against Oldsmobile whatsoever, but I've never owned one, and I don't think I'm going to own one in the future." By this time poor John was climbing the walls in frustration.

At the end of the season I came home and did some commercials—for free. I did one for Acadia Ambulance and I did one for USL, and I did one for the tourist and convention bureau.

Other commercial ventures have come up, and some I've accepted: One to be national spokesman for Burger King's Pitch, Hit and Run program. Even one for Dr Pepper. But at the same time I've seen what the banquets and commercials can do to a ballplayer, how the time it takes to do them can cause a husband to be away from his wife and children for days at a time, how the publicity and adulation can cause marriages to break up, and I've told John, "My family comes first. Whatever contract you negotiate, there has to be a clause in the contract that Bonnie and Jamie get to come with me and that they can come onto the commercial shooting site."

I could leave baseball tomorrow and not look back. I love baseball, but I don't need it. People who grow up in this area tend to stay here. It's the way of life, a tradition, a custom. Everything I need is here. If I want to go fishing tomorrow, I can go fishing. I may not come in with a big mess of fish, or if I go hunting I may not come back with a big bag of birds, but at least I am able to do these things, the things that are truly important to me.

If I wasn't playing baseball, I'd be just as happy living in Lafayette doing something else. I don't need interests in tennis clubs, sportswear, or restaurants. All I want is to be able to buy thirty acres of woodland with a muddy bayou running through the property where I could build a house, so that without leaving home I could take my shotgun out into the woods and hunt with Travis, Grandpa Gus, family or friends or just sit alone for hours under a tree listening to the sounds of life in the woods.

APPENDIX A

Ron Guidry's Favorite Cajun Recipes as Prepared by Bonnie Guidry

Chicken and Sausage Gumbo

4-5 pound fryer (cut up)
1 c. cooking oil
1 c. all-purpose flour
4 qt. water
1 large chopped onion
2 cloves of garlic chopped
1/2 c. green onion tops
salt, pepper to taste
1-2 pounds of smoked or fresh sausage

To make the roux, heat the oil in a heavy skillet. Add flour and stir constantly on medium heat until medium to dark brown. Remove and set aside. Season hen, then fry in a large pot in oil till light brown. While the chicken is cooking, boil the water in a large pot, adding the roux. Let the water boil between one and two hours. Add the chicken. Cook over low heat for about a half an hour. Add sausage and green onion. Season to taste. Let the gumbo cook about a half hour more.

Crabmeat Cobbler

1/2 c. margarine
1 small chopped green pepper
1 medium onion
1/2 c. sifted flour
1 teaspoon dry mustard
1/2 teaspoon accent
1 c. milk
1 c. shredded Cheddar cheese
1 c. crabmeat
1 No. 2 can of tomatoes drained
2 teaspoons of Worcestershire sauce
1/2 teaspoon salt

Melt the margarine, sauté the green pepper and onions until tender. Blend in flour, mustard, seasonings, milk, and cheese. Cook, stirring constantly until the cheese is melted. Add crabmeat, tomatoes, Worcestershire sauce, and salt. Pour into casserole.

Topping: Add one can biscuits. Place on top of casserole. Bake till biscuits are done. Or: Add bread crumbs and sliced Cheddar cheese to top of casserole and melt in oven.

Crawfish Étouffée

1 pound cleaned crawfish tails (reserve fat)
1 stick margarine
1 large onion chopped fine
1/2 large green pepper chopped fine
1/2 tablespoon flour

Sauté onions and pepper in margarine. Add flour. Cook till onions are tender. Add fat if available. Sir constantly. Cook 5 to 10 minutes. Add crawfish tails and just enough hot water for desired consistency. Simmer for 20 minutes. Serve over rice. Makes 2-3 servings.

Ron's Wild Duck Special
—recipe by Mrs. Joyce Matthews, Bonnie's mom.

6 (preferably wild) ducks cleaned
6 medium onions
3 cloves of garlic
6 large Irish potatoes
salt
red cayenne pepper
giblets of ducks (if available)

Day before cooking: Chop onion and garlic very fine. Season with salt and pepper. Pat ducks with vinegar. Slit two holes in breast of duck and stuff with onion-garlic mixture. Dice potatoes. Add more onion-garlic mixture. Stuff stomach and close with toothpicks. Sit ducks in covered pan with vinegar and seasoning and refrigerate overnight.

Next day: Put one cup cooking oil in large Dutch oven. Cook ducks till golden brown. Remove ducks from pan, add giblets, one-half cup onions. Cook about 15 minutes over low heat. Add ducks and 2 cups of water. Simmer about 2 hours. Serve over hot rice. Serves 6 adults (unless one of them is Ronnie, then it serves 3 adults).

Louisiana Pecan Pralines

1-1/2 c. dark brown sugar
1-1/2 c. granulated sugar
1/2 teaspoon salt
1 c. milk
1/4 teaspoon cream of tartar
1/2 stick margarine
1 teaspoon vanilla
2-1/2 c. pecan halves

Combine sugar, salt, milk, and tartar. Stir over low heat until sugar dissolves. (Scrape crystals from side of pan with rubber spatula.) Cook to soft ball stage, then cool slightly away from heat. Add margarine, vanilla, and pecans and beat until creamy. Drop by spoonfuls onto piece of *buttered* wax paper. Let cool before storing.

APPENDIX B

Lifetime Career Statistics

1978 Game by Game

Date	Opp.	IP	R	H	ER	BB	K	W	L	ERA	Score
4-8	Tex	7	1	6	1	2	2	0	0	1.29	1-2
4-13	CHI	9	2	10	2	2	3	1	0	1.69	4-2
4-18	BALT	6.2	3	7	3	2	4	1	0	2.38	4-3
4-24	Balt	7	1	6	0	2	2	2	0	1.82	8-2
4-30	Minn	6.1	2	3	0	4	7	2	0	1.50	3-2
5-5	TEX	6.1	1	5	1	5	7	3	0	1.49	5-2
5-13	kc	8	2	8	2	2	6	4	0	1.61	5-2
5-18	Clev	8.1	3	6	3	3	5	5	0	1.84	5-3
5-23	CLEV	9	1	5	1	2	11	6	0	1.73	10-1
5-28	TOR	9	3	6	3	0	6	7	0	1.88	5-3
6-2	Oak	8.1	1	6	1	2	11	8	0	1.80	3-1
6-7	Sea	9	1	6	1	2	10	9	0	1.72	9-1
6-12	OAK	9	0	3	0	2	11	10	0	1.57	2-0
6-17	CAL	9	0	4	0	2	18	11	0	1.45	4-0
6-22	Det	8	2	6	2	2	8	12	0	1.50	4-2
6-27	BOS	6	4	8	4	3	6	12	0	1.71	6-4
7-2	DET	8	2	6	2	2	6	13	0	1.75	3-2
7-7	Mil	6	5	8	5	1	3	13	1	1.99	0-6
7-14	CHI	9	6	8	6	3	10	13	1	2.23	7-6
7-20	Minn	9	0	4	0	3	8	14	1	2.11	4-0
7-25	kc	9	0	6	0	0	8	15	1	1.99	4-0
7-30	MINN	6.2	3	6	2	3	10	15	1	2.02	4-3
8-4	BALT	9	2	5	1	0	10	15	2	1.97	1-2
8-10	MIL	9	0	3	0	1	9	16	2	1.88	9-0
8-15	Oak	9	0	4	0	3	9	17	2	1.79	6-0
8-20	Sea	5	2	3	1	1	3	17	2	1.79	4-5
8-25	OAK	8	1	5	1	4	5	18	2	1.77	7-1
8-30	Balt	7	4	7	4	1	8	19	2	1.88	5-4
9-4	DET	9	1	5	1	3	8	20	2	1.84	9-1
9-9	Bos	9	0	2	0	4	5	21	2	1.77	7-0
9-15	BOS	9	0	2	0	3	5	22	2	1.71	4-0
9-20	Tor	1.2	5	6	3	0	1	22	3	1.81	1-8
9-24	Cle	9	0	2	0	1	8	23	3	1.74	4-0
9-28	TOR	9	1	4	1	1	9	24	3	1.72	3-1
10-2	Bos	6.1	2	6	2	2	5	25	3	1.74	5-4

(lower case team indicates road game)

ALCS

10-7	KC	8	1	7	1	1	7

WS

10-13	LA	9	1	8	1	7	4

Regular Season Totals

IP	R	H	ER	BB	K	W	L	ERA
273.2	61	187	53	72	248	25	3	1.74

Shutouts	Games	Complete Games
9	35	12

American League Eastern
Division Championship Game

(October 3, 1978 at Boston)

New York   **Boston**

	AB	R	H	RBI		AB	R	H	RBI
Rivers (cf)	2	1	1	0	Burleson (ss)	4	1	1	0
Blair (cf)	1	0	1	0	Remy 2b)	4	1	2	0
Munson (c)	5	0	1	1	Rice (dh)	5	0	1	1
Piniella (rf)	4	0	1	0	Yastrzemski (lf)	5	1	2	2
Jackson (dh)	4	1	1	1	Fisk (c)	3	1	1	0
Nettles (3b)	4	0	0	0	Lynn (cf)	4	0	1	1
Chambliss (1b)	4	1	1	0	Hobson (dh)	4	0	1	0
White (lf)	3	1	1	0	Scott (1b)	4	0	2	0
Doyle (2b)	2	0	0	0	Brohamer (3b)	1	0	0	0
Spencer (ph)	1	0	0	0	Bailey (ph)	1	0	0	0
Stanley (2b)	1	0	0	0	Duffy (3b)	0	0	0	0
Dent (ss)	4	1	1	3	Evans (ph)	1	0	0	0
	35	5	8	5		36	4	11	4

								R	H	E
New York	0 0 0	0 0 0	4 1 0					5	8	0
Boston	0 1 0	0 0 1	0 2 0					4	11	0

LOB—New York 6, Boston 9. Doubles—NY: Rivers, Munson; Bos: Scott, Burleson, Remy. Home runs—NY: Dent (5), Jackson (27); Bos: Yastrzemski (17). Stolen Base—NY: Rivers. Sacrifices—Bos: Brohamer, Remy.

Pitchers			IP	R	H	ER	BB	K
Guidry	W	(25-3)	6.1	2	6	2	1	5
Gossage			2.2	2	5	2	1	2
Torre	L	(16-13)	6.2	4	5	4	3	4
Stanley			.1	1	2	1	0	0
Hassler			1.2	0	1	0	0	2
Drago			.1	0	0	0	0	0

Save—Gossage (27). Passed Ball—Munson. Time—2:52. Attendance—32,925.

1978 Highlights

*Recorded Yankee record 13 straight wins to begin the season (2 short of A.L. record).

*Posted .893 winning percentage, the highest in baseball history by a 20-game winner.

*On June 17, he struck out 18 California Angels at Yankee Stadium to set a Yankee club record, and A.L. record for most strikeouts in a 9 inning game by a lefthander.

*248 strikeouts on the season, tied him for third in the Major Leagues with Phil Niekro, behind J.R. Richard and Nolan Ryan; it was second in the A.L.—the 248 strikeouts broke the Yankee single-season record previously set by Jack Chesbro in 1904 with 239.

*His 9 shutouts tied Babe Ruth's A.L. record for most shutouts by a lefthander set in 1917.

*Led the major leagues in wins (25), ERA (1.74), winning percentage (.893), and shutouts (9).

*15 of his 25 wins during the regular season followed a Yankee loss; his World Series win also followed a Yankee loss.

*American League Player of the Month in June and September.

*His 1.74 ERA is the second lowest in history by an A.L. lefthander to Dutch Leonard's 1.01 in 1914.

*His 1.74 ERA is the lowest by a lefthander since Sandy Koufax's 1.73 in 1966.

*Yanks won 30 of the 35 games that Guidry started this year, and in the 5 they lost, they scored only 7 runs.

*Ron won 12 of his last 14 regular-season decisions in 1978, including 7 shutouts; 3 of his last 5 wins were 2-hit shutouts.

*The American League batted .193 vs. Guidry this year, as opposed to .261 overall.

*Struck out 10 or more in a game 8 times.

CY YOUNG AWARD VOTING (5 pts for first, 3 for second, 1 for third)

	First	Second	Third	Points
GUIDRY	28	0	0	140

Lifetime Career Statistics

Year	Club	ERA	W-L	G	GS	CG	IP	H	R	ER	BB	SO	SV
1971	Johnson City	2.11	2-2	7	7	2	47	34	13	11	27	61	0
1972	Ft. Lauderdale	3.82	2-4	15	13	1	66	53	35	28	50	61	0
1973	Kinston	3.21	7-6	20	16	2	101	85	53	36	70	97	1
1974	West Haven	5.26	2-4	37	8	1	77	80	48	45	53	79	3
1975	Syracuse	2.86	6-5	42	0	0	63	46	24	20	37	76	14
	New York	3.38	0-1	10	1	0	15	15	6	6	9	15	0
1976	Syracuse	0.68	5-1	22	0	0	40	15	5	4	13	50	9
	New York	5.62	0-0	7	0	0	16	20	12	10	4	12	0
1977	New York	2.82	16-7	31	25	9	211	174	72	66	65	176	1
1978	New York	1.74	25-3	35	35	16	274	187	61	53	72	248	0
1979	New York	2.78	18-8	33	30	15	236	203	83	73	71	201	2
	M.L. Totals	**2.49**	**59-19**	**116**	**91**	**40**	**752**	**599**	**234**	**208**	**221**	**652**	**3**

CHAMPIONSHIP SERIES RECORD

Year	Club	ERA	W-L	G	GS	CG	IP	H	R	ER	BB	SO	SV
1976	New York (pr)	0.00	0-0	1	0	0	0	0	0	0	0	0	0
1977	New York	3.97	1-0	2	2	1	11.1	9	5	5	3	8	0
1978	New York	1.12	1-0	1	1	0	8.0	7	1	1	1	7	0
	L.C.S. Totals	**2.79**	**2-0**	**4**	**3**	**1**	**19.1**	**16**	**6**	**6**	**4**	**15**	**0**

WORLD SERIES RECORD

Year	Club	ERA	W-L	G	GS	CG	IP	H	R	ER	BB	SO	SV
1976	New York					(did not appear)							
1977	New York	2.00	1-0	1	1	1	9	4	2	2	3	7	0
1978	New York	1.00	1-0	1	1	1	9	8	1	1	7	4	0
	W.S. Totals	**1.50**	**2-0**	**2**	**2**	**2**	**18**	**12**	**3**	**3**	**10**	**11**	**0**

"One of the most absorbing books ever written on American business, and one of the most devastating."
The Denver Post

The Daring National Bestseller

ON A CLEAR DAY YOU CAN SEE GENERAL MOTORS

J. PATRICK WRIGHT

John Z. DeLorean was one of General Motors's fastest rising young executives, and in line to become the next president, when he decided to get out. His astonishing first-person account, written in collaboration with J. Patrick Wright, tells of corruption, mismanagement and irresponsibility that ranges from spying on automotive competitors, to substantial, and possibly illegal political contributions, to repeated rejections of proposals to build smaller, more fuel-efficient cars—largely because "we make more money on big cars."

"This book is the most devastating indictment of modern-day American business by an insider I have ever read." *Boston Globe*

"A rare look into the bowels of a major corporation ...riveting." *Chicago Sun-Times*

"Pizzazz and scoops to spare."
The Village Voice

AVON Paperback

51722 • $2.95

OACD 2-81 (2-A)